THE COMPLETE GUIDE TO SHETLAND SHEEPDOGS

Catrina Mehltretter

LP Media Inc. Publishing
Text copyright © 2021 by LP Media Inc.
For information address LP Media Inc. Publishing, 3178 253rd Ave. NW, Isanti, MN 55040
www.lpmedia.org

Publication Data

Catrina Mehltretter
The Complete Guide to Shetland Sheepdogs – First edition.
Summary: "Successfully raising a Shetland Sheepdog from puppy to old age" – Provided by publisher.
ISBN: 978-1-954288-00-3
[1. Shetland Sheepdogs – Non-Fiction] I. Title.

Design by Sorin Rădulescu
First paperback edition, 2021

TABLE OF CONTENTS

INTRODUCTION

A llow me to begin with two personal confessions. After all, if I'm asking you to trust the advice I give you, then in return, I need to be completely open and honest with you.

Confession #1: I am not a Sheltie expert. I have no formal training as a dog breeder or trainer. The knowledge that I do have has been gained though my personal experience as a Sheltie owner—namely, a lot of trial and error—as well as through books, articles, and conversations with various experts and fellow dog-owners. What I'm offering you is the compilation of

Photo Courtesy
of Catrina Mehltretter

everything I have learned, so you can have a head start in your own journey raising your Sheltie and hopefully be more prepared than I was.

Confession #2: I have the smartest, most adorable Sheltie in the world. She's taken. I'm sorry. However, don't let this knowledge dissuade you from pursuing your own dream of owning a Shetland Sheepdog. After all, if he's even half as good of a dog as mine, then he's going to be pretty incredible!

I am the proud dog mom of an eight-year-old Sheltie named Winnie. She was originally my husband's puppy, and I joke that I only married him so I could officially call her mine as well. When I first met her, she was just a tiny

Photo Courtesy
of Catrina Mehltretter

ball of fluff barking at me from under the table, and I fell in love immediately. I soon won her over, and now I like to tease my husband by saying I've replaced him as her favorite (although in reality, it's a close contest, which he usually wins).

Winnie is our baby. She can be frustratingly stubborn at times. She has a never-ending supply of energy and lives to play fetch. She has taken on the self-appointed role of alarm system, barking whenever we encounter anyone on our walks and alerting us whenever someone is outside our apartment. She is so sweet and gentle...and a bit of a scaredy-cat sometimes. She has the biggest heart and can always sense when either of us is sad or upset, and she will immediately come over to comfort us. She loves us unconditionally.

That is what you can expect from living with a Sheltie. Of course, not all Shelties are the same—they each have their own unique quirks and personality traits—but some universal characteristics and tendencies do exist within the breed. My hope is that learning about the Shetland Sheepdog breed in general will help you better understand your own Sheltie, thereby allowing you to develop a stronger relationship with your furry friend.

As with any relationship, it will have its ups and downs; however, the more prepared you are for the journey, the smoother it will be in the long run. Of course, Shelties aren't for everyone, but if you do determine this breed is the right fit for you, you'll find that raising a Sheltie can be a rewarding and fulfilling experience that will change your life for the better.

Good luck, and congratulations on adding a Sheltie to your family. It might be one of the best decisions you've ever made!

CHAPTER ONE
About The Shetland Sheepdog

The Shetland Sheepdog, also known as a Sheltie, is a small herding dog that resembles a miniature Collie. Shelties are intelligent, energetic, and loyal. Their gentle disposition makes them well-suited for families with children, and their natural athleticism helps them excel in agility competitions.

Photo Courtesy of Gaby Garcia

Photo Courtesy of Jan Buchner

History of the Shetland Sheepdog

"While the original Shelties had many names including 'Toonie do' the breed was officially accepted into AKC as the Shetland Collie. This name only lasted for a year before being changed to Shetland sheepdog due to complaints by the Rough Collie fanciers who felt the new breed wasn't worthy of sharing the same name. Ironically, now it is the Sheltie fanciers who get upset when their Shelties are called mini collies."

LINNEA GULSTAD
Sunny Shelties

Shetland Sheepdogs were originally bred as herding dogs in the Shetland Islands, a Scottish archipelago located in the northern extremity of the United Kingdom. The Shetland Islands are known for their small, hearty animals, including the Shetland Pony, and Shetland Sheepdogs were specifically bred to look after the sheep and miniature cattle that populated the islands. According to the American Shetland Sheepdog Association, the breed can be traced back to the Scottish Collie, King Charles Spaniel, Pomeranian, and other dogs indigenous to the islands, but the exact mix of these breeds is still unknown.

The breed was originally named the Shetland Collie, but protests from Collie breeders called for a greater distinction between the breeds, thus leading to the name being changed to Shetland Sheepdog. The Shetland Sheepdog's role also began to shift from farm animal to companion when visitors to the islands were enamored by these adorable fluffy dogs, and breeders recognized the potentially lucrative market in selling them as pets. The breed made its way to the United States in the early twentieth century, and it was officially recognized by the American Kennel Club in 1911.

Physical Characteristics

"Sheltie personalities vary, but their origins trace back to dogs that did it all: they helped keep the chickens where they belong, notified owners of visitors and/or intruders, and were small enough to be part of the home, not just a working breed. They were not city dogs, but they are highly adaptable to apartment living. The most important thing is that the Sheltie be part of the family, living in the home, and that it becomes a member of the family, not just a guard dog or ornament."

LAURA WILLSON
Wildwest Shelties

Almost everywhere we go, people stop my husband and me to comment that Winnie looks like a "mini Lassie," and it is a fitting description. Shelties are in many ways miniature versions of their larger cousin, the Rough Collie, but there are several significant distinguishing features. Shelties have a shorter, narrower muzzle, whereas the Rough Collie has a longer, broader face. Shelties also have a noticeably deeper curve between their eyes, making their eyes appear larger and brighter. The biggest difference is still the

Photo Courtesy of Andrea Porter

size comparison, though, for while Collies are often between 22-26 inches tall and weigh 50-75 pounds, depending on the gender, Shelties range from 13-16 inches tall and weigh 15-25 pounds.

It is also worth noting that there is a difference between American Shelties and English Shelties, specifically in the shape of the face. American Shelties tend to be on the larger side, with slightly longer, straighter faces. English Shelties, on the other hand, are usually smaller, with softer, more delicate features. I generally find that American Shelties look similar to Collies, whereas English Shelties have a more foxlike appearance.

Like Collies, Shelties have long, straight, dense fur, which is usually longer around the neck and chest like a mane and fades into shorter hair toward the back. They have long, fluffy tails, which typically hang low. Their fur can be three different color combinations: sable and white, with the sable ranging from golden to bright chestnut to a deep walnut color; black, tan, and white; or blue merle, tan, and white. The exact amount of tan and white can vary.

Their eyes are dark and oval shaped, except for the blue merle, which can have blue eyes. Shelties have very expressive faces, and their eyes are usually bright, intelligent, and curious. They will look alert and reserved toward strangers, but nothing compares to seeing your Sheltie look at you with eyes filled with love and gentleness.

Shelties' ears are floppy when they're puppies, but as they get older, the cartilage hardens, causing their ears to stand up straight. Breed standards mandate that the tips of the ears remain floppy, however, so many breeders and owners choose to "tip" their puppies' ears by preventing the cartilage from hardening completely. This is done by consistently holding or weighing down the tips of the puppy's ears between the ages of ten weeks and one year. If you do not plan to show your Sheltie professionally, this step is not necessary. It is a purely cosmetic procedure that allows the Sheltie to retain a more youthful, puppyish appearance. However, it also does not hurt the puppy or damage his hearing in any way, so the decision simply comes down to your own personal preference. If you do decide to tip your Sheltie's ears, there are a few possible methods:

1. **Gluing:** You can put a dab of glue on the tips of your Sheltie's ears to hold them down. It is important to make sure that whatever glue you choose is removable and nontoxic. Hair extension glue works well; this is what my husband used with Winnie. To use this method, put a small amount of glue on the outside of your Sheltie's ears at the very tips, roll them down slightly, and gently attach them to the top of your puppy's head. Hold for a couple minutes. (You might need help from a second person since your puppy will probably be squirmy.) Be careful not to fold the ears too much because that can cut off circulation and damage the ears.

The glue can last up to a few weeks, then you will need to remove any remaining glue using adhesive remover, wash it out, and repeat.

2. **Taping:** You can also use tape instead of glue to hold the ears down. Most people prefer using moleskin or Japanese tape. For this method, you will need to clean the inside of your Sheltie's ears using rubbing alcohol and cotton pads, then allow them to dry completely. This will remove any residue that might prevent the tape from sticking. Cut a strip of tape the length of the puppy's ear. Once the ear is dry, place the tape along the inside of the ear, from the bottom inside corner to where the hair starts at the tip. Next, cut another strip of tape, around an inch long, and create a roll with the sticky side out. Place the roll onto the tape already in the ear, around three-fourths of the way up the ear, and roll the tip of the ear onto it. Again, make sure the ear is not folded or pinched to the point where proper circulation might be affected. Repeat for the other ear.

The tape will need to be changed weekly; when removing, be gentle, use adhesive remover, and go from the bottom of the ear to the tip to avoid pulling the hair or skin too much.

3. **Weighting:** Some people weigh down the tips of their Sheltie's ears using a mixture of glue and Tungsten powder. Do NOT use lead or any other toxic materials. To use this method, mix a small amount of Tungsten powder with fabric glue and allow it to harden. Place a dab of glue on the very tip of the inside of the ears and attach the Tungsten mixture. This should gently weigh down the ears without hurting or straining them. You can adjust the amount of weight as necessary, but make sure both sides are even.

> **NOTE:** This method is controversial since some people think that weighting the ears will end up making the cartilage grow stronger, while others argue there is no scientific proof to support this claim. Some people also use this method as a temporary solution if they want to show a Sheltie whose ears have already hardened. Whether or not this would be deemed acceptable in place of truly tipped ears would depend on the rules of the individual dog show.

With any of these methods, STOP IMMEDIATELY if you notice any skin irritation or any other signs of distress. You should also consult with your vet if you have any questions or concerns about the process. Your puppy might be confused and curious what you did at first, but once you play with him and give him a treat, he shouldn't notice his ears or be bothered by them. Again, ear tipping is an elective cosmetic procedure; you don't have to do it at all if you don't want to. Your Sheltie can be perfectly happy and healthy whether his ears are floppy or pointed. You should simply do your research and decide what would be best for you and your puppy.

Photo Courtesy
of Anna Isaksson

Behavioral Characteristics

"The breed's love of family, especially children, is truly amazing. They look after them as if they were guarding a flock of sheep. They are gentle, loving, high energy and extremely intelligent."

SUZI BEACHAM
Shalamar Shelties

A Sheltie is one of the most intelligent dogs you will ever meet. This intelligence is a double-edged sword, however, for while this trait makes Shelties very bright and trainable, it also means they have a mind of their own and may become more stubborn once they decide they don't want to be told what to do. If trained properly, Shelties are very eager to please and are excellent candidates for obedience competitions, as well as (nearly) perfectly mannered members of your household. We will discuss proper training techniques in greater detail later on in this book.

Shelties are energic and playful, as well as loyal and affectionate with their family. They need to be kept entertained, and they crave attention and interaction. They are gentle in nature and very even tempered, which makes them excellent with children. They can be wary of strangers, though, which is why it is important to socialize them early. Shelties are also good watchdogs and will bark at any suspicious noises outside your home. Their bark is definitely worse than their bite, though, for their bite is practically nonexistent.

Shelties can be very sensitive. They are extremely cognizant of the mood of the household, and they will get nervous and stressed if you're angry or upset. They will also become concerned when you're sad or hurt and will likely try to comfort you. Shelties can also be rather skittish at times and sometimes have a strong sense of personal space. If you're looking for a lapdog, a

FUN FACT

America Shetland Sheepdog Association (ASSA)

The American Shetland Sheepdog Association (ASSA) was founded in 1929 at the Westminster Kennel Club show and is the American Kennel Club (AKC) Parent Club for the breed. As of 2020, the club consisted of 767 members and 66 member-breed clubs across the country. The four key objectives of the ASSA are to promote quality, encourage clubs, maintain a standard of excellence, and encourage sportsmanship. More information about the club and its events and membership can be found at www.americanshetlandsheepdogassociation.org.

Sheltie may not be the best choice for you. However, this varies from Sheltie to Sheltie; some can be quite cuddly. Either way, your Sheltie will not hesitate to let you know when he's in need of attention.

You'll know you're doing something right when your Sheltie sneezes. One of the most adorable Sheltie-specific mannerisms is that they sneeze when they get excited. For Winnie, this usually happens when we throw the ball for her or when we get home from work and give her lots of attention. Shelties will also prance when they're happy and bounce up and down with their front paws when feeling playful. Similarly, your Sheltie will likely "bow" to greet you or invite you to play and will melt your heart by smiling up at you, which is a sign of both contentment and submissiveness.

Overall, Shelties are generally gentle and submissive, intelligent and highly intuitive, loyal and affectionate, as well as energetic and agile. They make loving companions, excellent family dogs, and they are strong contenders for both obedience and agility competitions.

Is a Sheltie the Right Fit for You?

"The most important aspect of living with a Sheltie is your commitment. Shelties are a handler-oriented breed commonly called 'Velcro' dogs. They will follow you into the bathroom, lay at your feet or in your lap when you sit down and frequently demand attention. They can do well in an apartment with one person or live on a 100 acre farm with a big family as long as they are able to have quality, interactive time with their people. This can be learning new tricks, talking to them with eye contact, walks, cuddling on the couch, or making up new games. Shelties need to feel like a part of things and do best in homes where they get individual attention daily."

LINNEA GULSTAD
Sunny Shelties

Shelties are wonderful companions, but depending on the individual needs, desires, and expectations of each household, they may not be the best fit for everyone. Here are a few signs you should consider getting a different breed instead:

1. **You do not have a very active lifestyle.** Shelties are energetic and playful, and they need copious amounts of daily exercise. If you want a dog to lounge around the house with you all day, you may want to look for a different breed.

    NOTE: Shelties can do very well in small spaces. It doesn't matter if you live in a house or an apartment as long as you devote time to giving your Sheltie adequate exercise.

2. **You're not willing to put in the time for proper training.** Shelties are very intelligent and need adequate mental stimulation. They can also easily replace you as pack alpha if you let them, and they can fall into bad habits if they're bored.

3. **You have a problem with finding dog hair everywhere.** Shelties have two coats (yes, two—we'll explain that later) of fur, and they shed. A LOT. With proper grooming, this shedding can be mitigated, but you can still expect to find fluff all over your house. If you're allergic to dog hair or don't want to deal with shedding, a Sheltie is not the right choice for you.

Photo Courtesy of Liana Maloney

4. **You want a low-maintenance dog that you only need to bathe occasionally.** Shelties need to go to a professional groomer on a regular basis, in addition to being bathed and brushed at home.

5. **You need absolute silence.** Shelties are alert watchdogs and have the tendency to bark at noises or strangers outside their home. Although they are known for their high-pitched bark, they are typically not "yappy," and excess barking can be mitigated with training. However, this tendency is something to be aware of when debating whether a Sheltie is the right fit for you.

6. **You're not willing or able to devote time to giving lots of love and attention...** But in that case, you should probably consider getting a fish instead of a dog.

The ideal Sheltie owner is loving, active, and willing to offer gentle yet consistent training. If you're looking for a dog that's fun, affectionate, and always up for adventure—all in a small, adorable package—then a Sheltie may be the perfect match for you.

CHAPTER TWO
Choosing A Shetland Sheepdog

Once you decide to add a Sheltie to your family, the next logical question is where to get one. As with most dogs, there are two main options: buying or adopting. This is a debate that can become rather heated, and the slogan "Adopt, don't shop" has recently risen in popularity, shaming anyone who chooses to buy a puppy through a breeder rather than going to a shelter or rescue. After all, who wouldn't want to save a dog's life and offer a poor, homeless pup a loving family? Some people believe it is unethical to breed and sell puppies when there are so many dogs crowded in shelters, waiting to be loved, and they do make a strong argument. However, the issue is not as straightforward as it first appears, and there are several pros and cons to both sides.

Photo Courtesy of Rebecca Loyd

Photo Courtesy of Nadine Shortland

Before I continue, let me clarify that buying a puppy from a breeder is very different from buying a puppy from a pet store. I would highly recommend avoiding buying from a pet store for several reasons:

1. Most pet store puppies come from puppy mills. Even if the store claims the contrary, there is no way of knowing how honest this claim is, and ultimately, no reputable breeder will sell puppies to pet stores. Puppy mills are high-volume breeding facilities that ignore the health and well-being of the dogs and focus entirely on profit, churning out litter after litter, then abandoning or killing the parent dogs when they are no longer profitable.

2. Pet store puppies tend to have more health problems due to poor living conditions and poor breeding than puppies attained from a reputable breeder.

3. Pet store puppies also tend to have more behavioral issues due to poor socialization and poor breeding practices.

4. Although pet stores may claim the puppies are registered purebreds, breed standards are typically not upheld because the puppy mills focus entirely on quantity rather than quality.

One could argue that buying from a pet store is a way to rescue the puppies from the poor living conditions and give them a better life despite their unfortunate beginning. However, in the long run, this mentality only serves to promote and financially support the puppy mill industry. After all, where there is demand, this industry will maintain supply, and thousands of dogs will continue to pay the price.

Buying a Sheltie from a Breeder

"We believe that as a breeder, you should attempt to produces the healthiest puppy possible, and that you should strive to reach or exceed the breed standard set forth by each parent club. Each breed is predisposed to inherit genetic traits. We do various genetic testing on parents prior to breeding. For example these include OFA hips, OFA eyes, vWD, MDR1, DM etc. Shelties may be predisposed to have hip dysplasia, but it is uncommon. With genetic testing both parents, we know ahead of time if there is a problem & they are removed from our breeding program & retired into a loving pet home. We recommend families ask a breeder what testing has been done on the parents to ensure the healthiest puppy possible & what guarantees they might provide."

SHERRY DEEDS
BellaRose Shelties

Responsible breeders generally have smaller, often family-run businesses and genuinely care about their dogs, maintaining a high standard of living for the parent dogs and carefully screening any potential homes for their puppies. There are several reasons why someone might want to buy a Sheltie from a breeder, including:

1. **Wanting a specific breed.** The majority of shelter dogs are mixed breed, and while some shelters offer a waiting list for specific breeds, going to a breeder is often a faster, more direct route to finding a purebred Shetland Sheepdog. Breeders can also offer the genetic history of the puppy, and many are AKC certified and can provide paperwork and registration information.

2. **Wanting a puppy instead of an older dog.** Many people want a young puppy, so they can have the opportunity to bond with him and train him from an early age. While shelters and rescues do sometimes have puppies available, going through a breeder can again be a faster and easier option.

3. **Wanting to ensure the health of the puppy.** Breeders typically require thorough health screenings for their puppies and often offer a health guarantee, which I will explain shortly. Careful breeding and genetic testing can also act as safeguards against various hereditary health problems, which can develop later in the dog's life.

Financial concerns are probably the biggest deterrent from buying a puppy from a breeder, apart from the ethical desire to adopt a rescue dog instead. Raising a puppy is certainly a large investment no matter where the puppy comes from—given the cost of vet bills, supplies, etc.—but buying from a breeder can drastically increase the initial price. Purebred Shetland Sheepdog puppies can range from $800–2,000.

Photo Courtesy of Val Norris

How to Find a Reputable Breeder

"Shelties are supposed to show reserve towards strangers but not fear. Keep that in mind when first introduced to the dog. They should NEVER be aggressive! Buy from a reputable Breeder. Check for references, visit the facility if possible, make sure they do health checks and preferably a member in good standing with the American Shetland Sheepdog Association."

SUZI BEACHAM
Shalamar Shelties

If you simply Google "Shetland Sheepdog breeders near me," you'll likely be overwhelmed by the results. How do you know which one to pick? How do you know whom to trust? Unfortunately, not every breeder is responsible, so you need to learn how to identify which ones are reputable. Two good ways to narrow down the list are to go to the AKC Marketplace and look through their list of registered breeders or call your local veterinarian's office and ask for recommendations. Once you find a breeder you are interested in, here are a few basic guidelines to follow before making a final decision:

1. **Make sure you visit the breeder in person and see where the puppy lives**. Never buy a puppy online or agree to meet at an off-site location. If a breeder is pressuring you to meet off-site, this is a major red flag; he is likely hiding something.

   NOTE: When you're at the breeder's home or kennel, pay attention to how the dogs interact with each other, with you, and with the breeder. Are they friendly, playful, and sociable, or do they seem scared and hesitant to approach? Also, pay attention to how clean and spacious the overall environment is and how the breeder interacts with the dogs. Does he seem to genuinely care about them and interact with them lovingly, or does he seem distant and indifferent toward them, brushing them off and treating them like nuisances and/or commodities? Proper socialization is extremely important for the early development of the puppy, so you want to make sure the breeder is interacting with the puppies regularly and providing adequate mental and physical stimulation.

2. **While you're visiting the breeder's facility, make sure you meet the puppy's parents or at least the mother.** In addition to seeing how healthy and well taken care of the parents are, meeting them will give you the best idea of what your puppy will grow up to be in terms of

19

Photo Courtesy of Allana Kaminski

looks, size, and overall personality and demeanor. Of course, the puppy is not going to be a carbon copy of his parents, but genetics do play a significant role in determining how the puppy will look and act.

3. **Don't be afraid to ask questions.** Here are some questions you should ask:

   a. What health certifications and guarantees do you offer? Do the parents or grandparents have any health problems? What tests have you had done, for both the puppy and the parent dogs? Make sure you receive a full medical history for the individual puppy you are interested in.

   b. How many dogs do you own, and how often do you have puppies available? Responsible breeders keep their numbers small, typically specializing in only one or two breeds, and breed their dogs sparingly.

   c. Which puppy do you think would be a good fit for me? A good breeder will know the personalities of each puppy and will be able to make a recommendation for you based on your stated desires and needs.

   d. Any other questions or concerns you might have. There are no stupid questions—it's better to ask now than have problems arise later that might have been avoidable.

4. **Expect to be asked questions.** Responsible breeders will not sell their puppies to just anyone. They will ask questions, try to get to know you, and get a feel for what sort of environment you will provide the puppy. Some breeders will even conduct a home visit. If they do not think you would be a good fit for the puppy or have doubts about whether you would provide a loving home, they will not sell to you.

You may want to go back to visit the breeder multiple times, so you can get to know the personality of the puppy you are interested in and confirm that it is a good match. You also should not expect to show up and leave with a puppy. You will likely have to wait a few weeks after meeting the puppy for the first time before taking him home since puppies should not be separated from their mother until around eight weeks of age at the earliest. If a puppy is separated from his mother earlier than seven weeks old, he misses out on crucial developmental training, as interactions with his mother and littermates will teach the puppy how to be a dog, including appropriate play behavior. You will also need to allow time for any necessary health screenings and vaccinations before taking your puppy home.

Breeder Contracts and Guarantees

"Whether you buy from a breeder or a rescue make sure you review any contract carefully. Both should offer a clause that they can take the dog back at anytime or assist to rehome. Check if there is a spay/neuter clause and at what age that must occur. Sometimes taking an obedience class is required, ad check what health guarantees there are. Don't sign a contract with a rescue or a breeder unless you agree with it."

LINNEA GULSTAD
Sunny Shelties

A responsible breeder will likely require you to sign a contract. The main purpose of this contract is to serve as a reminder of your responsibilities as an owner and act as a guarantee that the puppy will have a good home.

Unless the puppy is show quality and is going to be bred, the breeder will likely require that you neuter or spay your puppy when they are around a year old. This is to prevent any accidental litters from being born. The puppy will likely only be bred if he exemplifies ideal breed standard, in which case you will need to speak with the breeder to make plans for future breeding once the puppy matures.

Responsible breeders will also require that you return the puppy to them in the event that the situation does not work out and the puppy needs to be rehomed. Of course, this scenario is not ideal, but various unexpected circumstances may arise that might prevent you from keeping the puppy, such as allergies, a move, or financial hardships. In these cases, the breeder would rather be the one to find the puppy a new home, so he can carefully screen the new owner, just as he did with you. If you end up giving the puppy to a friend or relative, the breeder will likely want to be notified of this change as well.

Many breeders include a health guarantee, which offers to replace your puppy or sometimes refund your money if he is discovered to have a congenital health condition covered by the guarantee, usually within a specific time frame. However, a puppy is not a toy you can just return to the store when you discover it's defective. By the time the health problem is discovered, you will have probably bonded with the puppy already and won't want to give him up. For this reason, these guarantees usually do not pose much of a threat to the breeder, but they are still worth being aware of in case of any serious problems.

Health Certifications and Testing

"One of the most important things in choosing a Sheltie is to get one from a breeder who cares about health, temperament, and function as well as beauty. Does the breeder do health testing? Not just a vet visit, but available genetic tests, vet ophthalmologist eye exams, and x-rays of the joints to determine correct conformation? Does the breeder pay attention to temperament and try to mix together the perhaps shyer dog with a more outgoing temperament, or the very active Sheltie with a calmer one? Do the dogs move well without a lot of rolling and flailing feet? Is the litter whelped in the house and raised underfoot so that they become accustomed to household noises?"

LAURA WILLSON
Wildwest Shelties

Most puppies will come with a health certification. The specifics of this certification vary by state, but this generally means the puppy has received all initial shots, has been dewormed, and has been examined by a veterinarian and deemed healthy at the time of sale.

In addition to providing health certifications, reputable breeders will conduct health tests to screen for any genetic conditions the breed might be prone to develop. For Shelties, the AKC requires a hip evaluation and an ophthalmologist (eye/vision) evaluation. While the puppies should be evaluated by a certified veterinarian to check for any outstanding health problems, they will likely be too young for any congenital conditions to be visible. This is why it is important for the puppies' parents to be tested as well.

A proper hip evaluation involves taking x-rays of the dog's hips in an extended position and sending the radiographs to be evaluated by a qualified organization, such as the OFA (Orthopedic Foundation for Animals). While any veterinarian can take the x-rays, your local vet will probably not be trained to properly read the results. The results will also not be accurate if the dog is younger than two years old, with the exception of PennHIP (University of Pennsylvania Hip Improvement Plan) testing, which involves a more complex series of imaging and requires the dog to be heavily sedated during the examination. PennHIP testing can only be performed by specially certified veterinarians, but it is often more accurate than OFA testing and can be done as early as sixteen weeks of age. Overall, the goal is to screen for the potential development of osteoarthritis (a degenerative joint disease that is extremely painful and can become crippling to the dog) and canine hip dysplasia (a condition in which the hip joint fails to function properly, resulting in pain and eventually the loss of function in the joint).

Shelties can also be prone to various eye diseases, such as Collie eye anomaly, where part of the eye is malformed, and progressive retinal atrophy, which can cause vision problems. There is no cure for either of these conditions, and dogs that have them are typically not bred. To test for these conditions, a certified veterinary ophthalmologist will conduct an eye exam and check for any anomalies. The results do not guarantee that there will not be any future problems, but they will give a better idea of what to expect.

Still, even if the testing shows that the puppy may develop a specific health condition, this does not necessarily mean you should not buy the puppy. The purpose of the testing is to make you aware of any potential problems before they arise, so you can be properly prepared. In some cases, early intervention can also help minimize the effects of the condition. If you do buy or adopt a puppy with known health risks, talk to your vet, make sure he or she is aware of the condition, and ask what steps you should take in managing the puppy's health and overall wellbeing.

Photo Courtesy of Melissa Burke

Adopting a Shetland Sheepdog

"If adopting from a rescue; make sure you have a vet reference and familiarize yourself with their policies before viewing their available dogs. Some rescues have strict requirements such as in home interviews, and only adopt to people who have a fully fenced yard."

LINNEA GULSTAD
Sunny Shelties

Of course, rather than going through a breeder who intentionally breeds litters of puppies to sell, you can instead adopt a homeless Sheltie in need of a family. Dogs are put up for adoption for a wide variety of reasons, including owner surrender—due to landlord issues, moving, behavioral issues, etc.—breeders going out of business or retiring their dogs, or dogs being rescued from an unsafe situation. While shelter dogs are typically mixed breed, around 25% of pets in shelters are purebreds, according to the Humane Society of the United States. There are also many breed-specific rescue organizations, so adopting a purebred Shetland Sheepdog is certainly an option.

It's worth clarifying the difference between a shelter and a rescue. Shelters can be privately or publicly funded, and they have a physical location you can visit where the animals are housed in various rooms or kennels. They typically have a variety of cats and dogs available for adoption, as well as

SHELTIES ON SOCIAL MEDIA
Luca the Sheltie

Luca the Sheltie enjoys a following of nearly 74,000 people on Instagram. This Norwegian Sheltie is an ambassador for I Love Dogs.no, a retailer for dog-related goods based in Norway. Luca's Instagram feed is full of picturesque portraits in the beautiful Scandinavian outdoors. Find him on Instagram @ lucathesheltie.

occasionally other types of animals. The main advantages of going to a shelter rather than a rescue are that you can walk through the facility and meet all the available pets before making your decision, and the adoption process is usually faster. However, due to limited resources and the kennel-like housing situation, the dogs are typically not as well socialized, and sometimes even friendly, well-mannered dogs can appear scared and stand-offish due to the crowded, unfamiliar environment.

Rescue organizations, on the other hand, are almost all funded privately through donations, and most operate either out of a single home or through a network of foster homes. Due to being in a home environment, the dogs are often better socialized and more relaxed, and the foster family will be able to provide more detailed information about the dog's habits and personality. The foster family is also typically more attached to the dog and therefore more concerned with ensuring that his forever home will be a good fit for him. As a result, the adoption process is often harder and more time-consuming than adopting from a shelter, which can be a turn-off for some people.

There are several pros and cons to adopting a Sheltie rather than going through a breeder. I'll start with the potential disadvantages:

1. **There are a lot of unknowns.** Shelter and rescue dogs typically have little to no known history, so you don't have the advantage of all the genetic tests offered by a breeder. This means the dog might have health issues which you don't know about. You also may not know the details of the dog's upbringing—how well socialized he was as a young puppy, whether he was abused, etc.—which can influence the dog's behavior.

2. **Possible behavioral problems.** If the dog was rescued from an unsafe situation, such as a puppy mill or an abusive home, he will likely be scared of people, at least at first. He also may not know how to interact with other dogs, and he may have other behavioral issues due to past trauma. He also may not be properly house-trained.

3. **Lack of availability.** As addressed previously, it can be harder to find a puppy to adopt since most shelter and rescue dogs are older. It can also be harder to find a purebred Sheltie unless you go through a Sheltie-specific rescue.

However, there are also many wonderful things about adopting a shelter or rescue dog, including but not limited to:

1. There are so many great dogs in need of a home who just want a family to love and be loved by. Some of these dogs were surrendered by their family through no fault of their own, and some just want to know what it's like to be loved by a human for the first time.

2. There can be advantages to adopting an older dog. Not everyone is well-suited to raise a puppy. While puppies are tiny, adorable, and lovable, they are also full of energy and require a lot of time and energy to train and care for. Depending on your schedule, you may not be able to accommodate these needs. While older dogs also require time, attention, and exercise, they are often more laid back and do not need to be constantly entertained, which might be ideal if you have a busy schedule. Plus, an older dog might already be house-trained. Older dogs are also still trainable, despite the old proverb stating otherwise. Shelties, in particular, maintain their intelligence and desire

Photo Courtesy of Rebecca Loyd

for mental stimulation even as they age—although you might have to fight against some bad habits if they're used to being in charge. Overall, an older dog can make a loving and faithful companion and is just as deserving of a forever home as a puppy.

3. Adoption fees are often significantly less expensive than buying from a breeder. Fees typically range from around $75–500 depending on the age and background of the dog. Sometimes adoption fees will cover the cost of initial vaccinations and spaying or neutering.

4. You could be saving a life—quite literally. The Humane Society of the United States estimates that three million cats and dogs are euthanized in shelters each year, and around 80% of these pets were healthy or treatable and could have been adopted. The problem is shelters are often overpopulated, so they sacrifice some of the animals that aren't adopted to make room for others. When you adopt from a shelter, you are not only saving the life of the animal you are adopting, but you are also improving the chances of adoption for the other animals within the shelter.

Shelter and rescue dogs aren't for everyone. You need to keep in mind the specific needs of your family, do your research, and decide what is best for you. For example, a rescue dog that has been abused and is easily frightened and potentially aggressive would probably not be the best fit for a family with young children. A different rescue dog might be a perfect match, or you might decide a puppy from a breeder is a better fit, in which case you should not feel ashamed. Every situation is different, and ultimately, the important thing is that you give your new Sheltie a loving home, no matter where he came from.

Adopting Littermates

When you go to the breeder or rescue to pick out your Sheltie, it can be difficult to choose just one puppy. After all, you might want your Sheltie to have a friend, and what better friend could he have than his own brother or sister? However, there are some important factors to consider before adopting littermates, and you shouldn't make an impulse decision simply because you don't want to leave one of the puppies behind. There are some advantages to adopting more than one puppy, including:

1. The puppies can be playmates. Puppies have boundless energy, and letting them play with each other and wear themselves out will save you the time and energy of entertaining them. Plus, it's adorable to watch two puppies wrestle and play together!

2. The puppies can keep each other company. Having a companion can help your puppy feel less lonely, especially if you're not able to be around all the time.

3. Littermates are already used to each other, so they might get along better than puppies from separate litters. (However, in some cases, littermates can end up becoming more aggressive toward each other, especially if they're the same gender.)

Still, there are also several reasons why adopting littermates can be a bad idea and why many experts recommend against it:

1. Littermates can become very closely bonded, to the extent that they do not end up bonding with anyone else, including you. This is known as littermate syndrome. In this scenario, the puppies are not well socialized, so they are excessively fearful when meeting new people or any dog that isn't their sibling. They will also have extreme separation anxiety whenever they are apart.

2. Training littermates can be very difficult. After all, why would they want to listen to you when they can just play with each other? It is recommended to train the puppies separately, so they don't distract each other, which will require double the time and work on your part.

3. Potty training littermates can also be more complicated. Housetraining in general is a time-consuming and often challenging task. Trying to keep track of two puppies and their potential bathroom signals, as well as taking them both outside when necessary, will double the work involved.

4. All costs are doubled, including initial adoption fees, supply costs, and future vet bills.

If you end up getting littermates, experts recommend you keep the puppies separated for substantial portions of the day, except for set play times. This will allow each puppy to bond with you and learn independence, which will hopefully prevent the development of littermate syndrome. It is also important for the puppies to be socialized with other dogs and not just with each other.

Overall, adopting littermates will double the amount of time, work, and money involved in raising them; however, only you can decide whether it's worth the investment. Just make sure you know what you're getting yourself into beforehand, and if you do decide to adopt littermates, make sure you properly train and socialize them to prevent future problems.

Choosing the Perfect Pup

"Every Sheltie puppy needs a person or family that suites that individual dog. Shelties have big hearts and can feel and react to their owner's emotions and health. They need understanding and love and will return just all of that if given a chance. We believe it's very important to match each individual dog to the right home."

WANDA FLETCHER
Serenity Shelties

I want you to take some time to sit and seriously consider what you are looking for in a dog. How would your ideal canine companion look and act? Do you want a big dog or a small dog? Do you want a dog that's playful and energetic, or do you want one that will simply sit with you and provide companionship? Do you want a dog that you can roughhouse with, or would you prefer a dog that's gentler and softer? Once you come up with these answers, you might want to go back and reread part of Chapter One to see whether the description of your preferred dog lines up with a Sheltie.

Next, consider your lifestyle. How many hours a day do you work, and how long are you typically away from home? Do you have children, and if so, how old are they? Do you enjoy hiking and going on walks, or are you more of a Netflix-and-chill type of person on your days off? Again, refer back to Chapter One to determine whether a Sheltie's personality matches your needs.

Photo Courtesy of Jennifer Lavers

You will also need to figure out your budget and how much you're willing to invest in a dog—for initial adoption costs as well as any future expenses. You will need to keep all these consider-ations in mind when choosing a Sheltie. After all, making sure you are a good fit for the dog is just as important as making sure the dog is a good fit for you.

This is the mindset you should have as you decide between breeders, shelters, and rescues, as well as when it's time to pick out a dog or puppy. There is no one-size-fits-all "perfect Sheltie." Shelties have unique person-alities, and what would be ideal for one person might be a deal-breaker for someone else.

For example, Winnie can be rather shy, and she gets nervous when we get too close to her. She doesn't like being held, and she prefers being petted from a safe distance. We love her quirks and respect her boundaries (well, mostly—my husband still tries to hold or hug her sometimes, which is one of the reasons I'm still in the running for her favorite); however, for someone who wants a cuddly lapdog, this would not be a good fit. This is why you should visit any dog you are interested in owning several times in order to understand his personality, as well as ask the breeder, shelter workers, or foster parents what their experience with the dog has been like.

It is also important to note that what might be a red flag for other breeds might not apply to Shelties. Specifically, with most dogs, you might want to avoid ones that are overly skittish and hang back barking rather than approaching you with a friendly and excited attitude. However, with Shelties, wariness is often normal behavior when meeting a stranger. Shelties can be shy and mistrusting of new people, and they might take a little while to warm up to you. However, they should eventually relax, and the initial meeting should become easier with each visit. This is also where talking to the care-taker can be helpful in giving you a better idea of how the Sheltie acts with someone he is comfortable with.

Once you find the perfect match for your home and decide to add him to your family, congratulations! You now have a best friend who will love you and bring so much joy to your life...and now you just have to figure out how to take care of him.

CHAPTER THREE
Preparing Your Home For Your Sheltie

Welcoming a new Sheltie into your family is a major, life-changing event, and you need to make sure you are properly prepared. This involves being aware of any potential dangers in your house that could hurt the puppy, making sure you have adequate space ready for your pup both inside and outside your house, and ensuring your children are prepared to welcome their new furry sibling.

Photo Courtesy of Teresa Lenhardt

Potential Household Dangers

Before bringing home your Sheltie, you need to be aware of anything in your home that could pose a threat to your pup and do any necessary "puppy-proofing" in preparation for your Sheltie's arrival. Let's walk through the house.

KITCHEN

First, the most obvious risk is food. Many food and beverage items intended for humans can be poisonous for dogs, including:

- Chocolate
- Coffee / Tea / anything caffeinated
- Avocadoes
- Grapes / Raisins
- Macadamia nuts
- Onions
- Garlic
- Raw, undercooked, or spoiled meat
- Xylitol (an artificial sweetener, often found in sugar-free gum and candy)
    NOTE: Check peanut butter for this ingredient before giving to a dog.
- Raw yeast dough
- Alcohol
- Salt

None of these foods should ever be fed to your dog or kept within his reach. Additionally, make sure your Sheltie stays out of the garbage, as moldy or rotting food can contain harmful bacteria that will poison him.

As a general rule, cleaning products should be stored somewhere safe where your Sheltie cannot access them. These products often contain dangerous chemicals that should never be ingested, by a human or a dog. Read the label before using any of these products and follow any applicable directions. Some products will specify that they should not be used near pets or children, in which case you will need to keep your Sheltie away from the area until it is completely dry and free of fumes.

Rat or mouse poison should also never be placed anywhere your Sheltie might consume it since this could cause serious or potentially life-threatening illness.

BATHROOM

One of the biggest risks in the bathroom is your medications. Human medications should never be consumed by dogs, whether they are prescription or not. Even over-the-counter medications, such as Tylenol, Ibuprofen, or cold medicines, can be dangerous for your Sheltie. Vitamins and diet pills intended for humans should also never be given to a dog. All these bottles need to be tightly closed and stored out of reach of your Sheltie.

You should also be aware of any trash in the bathroom. This is Winnie's biggest weakness. She's typically very well behaved and does not get into anything she shouldn't, except for the bathroom trashcan. She loves to tear up any tissues she finds in the trash and leave them scattered throughout the living room, so we have to be careful to close the bathroom door before we leave the house. You should be mindful that if any of the trash items are consumed, they can cause gastro-intestinal problems since they can be difficult to digest, in addition to being potential choking hazards. Things such as cotton balls, Q-tips, tampons, and dental floss can pose a higher risk in this regard.

Other potential risks in the bathroom include soaps and toothpaste, which should never be eaten by dogs. You will need to keep the toilet lid closed to prevent your Sheltie from drinking the water, which could irritate his stomach due to bacteria. You should also avoid using automatic toilet cleaning products, so your Sheltie will not be harmed by the chemicals in case the lid is accidentally left open.

LIVING ROOM & BEDROOM

The main things you will need to watch for in the living room and bedrooms are small objects that might be tempting for your Sheltie to eat. Think of your puppy as a curious toddler who will put absolutely anything in his mouth and try to eat it. This can include children's toys with small parts, such as Legos, as well as miscellaneous items, such as buttons, coins, or string. Batteries can be particularly dangerous for a dog to chew or swallow due to the chemicals they contain. Your puppy may also be tempted to chew on electrical cords, such as phone chargers, which can be dangerous for the puppy in addition to being frustrating for you.

These rooms also tend to contain various candles and diffusers to make the house smell nice. As the use of essential oils has become more popular, concerns have also been raised about the potentially harmful effects these oils can have on pets. While some claim that diffusing these oils in your home is dangerous for dogs, most people generally agree that diffusing nontoxic essential oils for a limited amount of time is fine as long as there is enough space and ventilation to prevent the smell from becoming too concentrated. However, certain essential oils are toxic for a dog to consume, such as cinnamon, citrus, pennyroyal, peppermint, pine, sweet birch, tea tree (melaleuca), wintergreen, and ylang ylang[1]. It is also generally best to avoid applying essential oils directly to your dog's skin, at least without consulting your vet.

YARD & GARAGE

The garage is home to many toxic substances, such as antifreeze, paint, and gasoline. Products such as pesticides, fertilizers, and weed killers also need to be stored safely. After these chemicals have been applied to the lawn or garden, you will need to keep your pet inside, or at least away from the application site, for the amount of time recommended on the label. Cocoa mulch can also be dangerous if ingested, and the salt used on icy driveways can irritate paws and can be poisonous if licked or eaten.

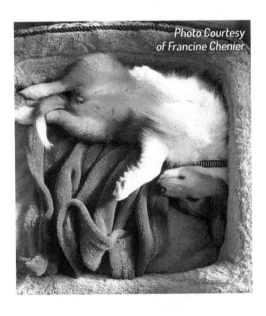

Photo Courtesy of Francine Chenier

Additionally, there are many common plants that can be poisonous for pets, such as azaleas, rhododendrons, tulip and daffodil bulbs, hyacinth, sago palms, and certain types of lilies. Of course, you probably won't want your dog to snack on your flowers in general, but you should keep an extra close eye on your Sheltie when he is around these plants.

---

1   List provided by Anna Burke, AKC, www.akc.org/expert-advice/health/are-essential-oils-safe-for-dogs.

Help! My Sheltie Ate Something Bad!

My intention in listing these potential dangers is not to overwhelm you with all the things that might hurt your beloved pet. I just want you to be aware of these risks, so you can hopefully prevent any potential problems. In most cases, if you use common sense and employ a few basic precautions, you should be fine. However, what happens if your Sheltie gets into something he shouldn't?

First, what are the signs your Sheltie has eaten something dangerous? Symptoms of food poisoning in dogs include:

- Vomiting
- Diarrhea
- Lethargy
- Convulsions / Tremors
- Blood in stool
- Labored breathing
- Excess drooling
- Loss of appetite

If you notice any of these signs, call your vet ASAP. If your veterinary office is closed, call the nearest 24-hour veterinary hospital. They will be able to give you instructions on what to do in your specific situation and will likely ask you to bring in your Sheltie to be examined. They may try to induce vomiting or administer activated charcoal to absorb the toxins. NEVER try to induce vomiting on your own unless explicitly instructed by your vet. At home, you should simply try to keep your Sheltie hydrated and, if the harmful substance is on his fur, try to keep your Sheltie from grooming himself.

You might also need to call your vet if your Sheltie ate something other than food, even if it isn't toxic. As gross as it sounds, you'll need to pay attention to your dog's bowel movements, and if there are any problems or if the object doesn't come out, he may require surgery to remove any obstructions.

SHELTIES IN FILM
The Adventures of Ragtime

The 1998 family film *The Adventures of Ragtime* features a miniature horse and a Sheltie. The Sheltie was owned by the associate producer of the film, Patty Fairchild, and was named Taylor. This Sheltie starred alongside Shelley Long, Jay Thomas, Perry King, and Justin Cooper.

Preparing Space for Your Sheltie

"I don't know that Sheltie puppies are all that different from other breeds when it comes to preparing the home. Puppies love to chew things so have appropriate substitutes available if they decide a chair leg is what they thing will satisfy their urge. New owners needs to be sure that shoes, socks, and other small articles are put away or put up where the puppy cannot get to them. New owners should learn about crate training and create managed space within their home so that puppy learns what is appropriate in that space. As they learn the boundaries and house-training, that space can be expanded."

LAURA WILLSON
Wildwest Shelties

Now that I have you adequately paranoid about all the potential poisons in your house, let's talk about creating a safe space for your Sheltie within your home.

First, you'll need to invest in a dog crate, which will provide a safe place for your Sheltie to sleep and stay when you have to run an errand—at least until you're comfortable leaving him home alone in the house. We will discuss crate training in Chapter Five, as well as explain how the crate can make potty training easier. The crate should be big enough for the Sheltie to comfortably stand and turn around in, but not too big, since the purpose is to provide a sense of security and to prevent the puppy from going to the bathroom where he sleeps. Some people suggest buying a new crate every few months as the puppy grows, but you could also simply buy a crate with a divider so you can adjust the size as necessary. Since Shelties are extremely sensitive and crave comfort, I would also highly recommend buying a dog bed or blankets to put in the kennel. After all, how would you like sleeping on a metal or plastic floor every night?

It can also be helpful to section off a "puppy-safe" area in your house using baby gates, especially if you're not able to keep a close eye on the puppy. Ideally, this area should have hard wood or tile floors, if possible, to make cleaning up any accidents easier and to protect your carpets. The puppy should have access to his kennel, where he can go to feel safe, as well as plenty of toys to keep him entertained.

If you're not able to section off a designated area for your puppy, you'll need to watch him more carefully and keep any doors closed to rooms where he could get himself into trouble. You'll also need to keep your shoes, belts, and anything else you don't want turned into a chew toy out of reach for a while.

As mentioned previously, Shelties can be well-suited for apartment living as long as they are given adequate daily exercise. It doesn't matter how big your home is; the important thing is that your Sheltie is kept safe and happy.

"We recommend ensuring that your yard has some kind of fencing up. Shelties love to run! They especially like chasing things with wheels, so having an adequate fence will make sure they are kept safe."

SHERRY DEEDS
BellaRose Shelties

Outdoor Spaces

Of course, having a fenced-in yard is ideal to allow your Sheltie to run and play freely, but you can always provide alternative forms of exercise through walks and indoor fetch if a yard is not an option. If you live in an apartment complex, you will need to make sure there are places where you can safely go on walks and enough grassy areas for your Sheltie to do his business.

However, if you are fortunate enough to have a yard, you should make sure it is completely fenced in before allowing your Sheltie to go outside unleashed. Even a fully mature Sheltie cannot be trusted to stay in a yard without a fence or leash. The Sheltie's strong herding instinct makes him prone to bolting when he notices movement, so if there is a squirrel across the street or a child riding a bike past the house, the Sheltie will run after them. This puts him at high risk of getting lost or hit by a car, so it is your responsibility to make sure your Sheltie stays where it is safe.

The fence must be at least four feet tall and fully reach the ground, and there should not be any gaps your Sheltie might squeeze through. Shelties are typically not prone to digging under fences; however, due to the wide variety of tendencies Shelties can exhibit, this may vary depending on the dog.

I would strongly caution against using an invisible fence. While invisible fences can be convenient, they are not always effective, particularly for Shelties. There's a good chance your Sheltie's desire to run after a bunny will overcome his fear of getting shocked, although nervousness about being shocked again might prevent him from returning home. For this reason, many Sheltie rescues stipulate on their application that they will not allow anyone who plans to use an electric fence to adopt one of their dogs. Additionally, if you live in an area with foxes or other predatory animals, the lack of a proper physical barrier may leave your Sheltie vulnerable to attack.

Photo Courtesy of Hope Meadows

Preparing Your Children for Your Sheltie's Arrival

Welcoming a new puppy into the home can be a big adjustment for a child, especially if he has not had any previous experience with dogs. The most important thing for your child to know before you bring home your Sheltie is how to treat a dog gently. This includes not chasing the dog around as well as petting him softly. Shelties are loving and gentle, and it is highly unlikely that they would ever intentionally hurt a child; however, they are extremely sensitive and can be quite skittish. If your Sheltie learns that your child will chase him or be rough with him, he will learn to avoid the child, and once this habit is formed, it will be hard to break. In order to foster a good relationship between Sheltie and child, you will need to teach your child how to interact with a Sheltie before you bring the puppy home.

Photo Courtesy of Lindsey Nielsen

You can model how to pet a dog softly using your child's stuffed animals, and if possible, it would be helpful to visit a friend's dog to give the child first-hand experience. You can remind the child to use "gentle hands," even if your friend's dog doesn't mind being petted more roughly, and remind the child to wait for the dog to approach willingly rather than chasing after him. Your child needs to be able to exhibit empathy ("You wouldn't like it if someone hit you, right? Ouch! That hurts!") and understand personal space and boundaries, which will require patience. Of course, you can't expect your child to grasp

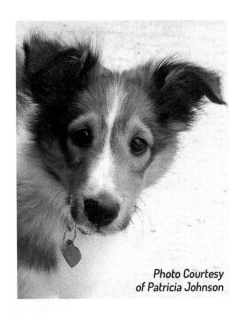

Photo Courtesy of Patricia Johnson

these concepts right away, but as you model appropriate behavior and correct any undesirable actions, he will eventually learn how to interact with your Sheltie, which will allow them to develop a strong friendship.

Chances are you'll have to be more worried about your children hurting your Sheltie than the other way around. However, you will still need to make sure your children understand that a puppy's teeth and nails are sharp, and they might accidentally get scratched or nipped while playing. While Shelties typically do not bite down, puppies can be rather mouthy when they play, which might be surprising or scary to a child who is not expecting it. You will also need to teach your child how to firmly say "No" when the puppy misbehaves. After all, the puppy will need to learn to obey both you and your child.

Your child will likely enjoy the opportunity to help take care of the puppy. Even young children can contribute to tasks, such as feeding the puppy or refilling his water dish. Older children and teenagers will be able to participate more in the training process, take the puppy for walks outside, and of course, play with the puppy and give him attention. Before buying your child a puppy and expecting him to take full responsibility for the puppy's care, however, you need to make sure that your child is mature enough to handle this task—unless you are willing and prepared to take over. You will also need to clarify ahead of time whose responsibility it will be to clean up the puppy's messes since your child will probably not volunteer for this job.

Overall, Shelties are fantastic family dogs and will interact gently with children of all ages. The children just need to be properly taught to treat the Sheltie gently in return.

CHAPTER FOUR
Bringing Your Sheltie Home

"Shelties aren't just dogs. They are family members and friends with no social boundaries who will follow you into the bathroom and gaze adoringly at you. They have an innate understanding That their job is to monitor location of their people at all times. To achieve this they typically sleep leaning against doors or touching a person so they are alerted if you leave."

LINNEA GULSTAD
Sunny Shelties

Photo Courtesy
of Paula Reid

T he long-anticipated day is finally here! After visiting your puppy numerous times and dreaming about his arrival, it's finally time to bring your
puppy home! All your preparations are complete. Now, all you have
to do is run through your final checklist one last time and try to ensure your
Sheltie's transition into your home is as seamless as possible.

Supplies to Have Ready

*"Your new Sheltie puppy will most likely just have been taken from its
litter mates, so giving them lots of fluff toys or warm blankets can help to calm
them through the first few nights."*

ROSE MARIE DORAN
Granite Gables Shetland Sheepdogs

While a loving home is the most important thing your Sheltie needs,
he will require a few material possessions as well. Here is a list of essential
items you need to have ready before you bring home your Sheltie:

1. **Water Bowl:** While technically any bowl will work, I would recommend
   finding one heavy enough to not tip over, or one that has a suction cup on
   the bottom, or else you will likely end up with water spilled everywhere.

2. **Food Bowl:** Again, the requirements aren't very picky. All your Sheltie really needs is a bowl that can hold food. However, if you find that he is in-
   haling the food rather than properly chewing it and ending up with stomach problems as a result, you will want to buy a slow-feeder bowl. This is
   a bowl specially designed to make the food harder to reach, so the dog
   is forced to slow down and only eat a little at a time, which will prevent
   bloating and indigestion. These bowls only cost around $8 on Amazon.

3. **Food:** Ask the breeder or current caretaker what food your Sheltie has
   been eating and buy the same type. Changing your dog's food suddenly
   can cause stomachaches, and Shelties, in particular, tend to have sensitive bellies. If you want to change brands later, you can transition slowly
   by mixing the food together before switching over entirely.

4. **Collar / Harness:** You will need to buy a comfortable collar. When you
   put this collar on the puppy, it should be loose enough to fit two fingers
   underneath. Remember, the collar should be snug enough that he can't
   slip out of it but loose enough that he doesn't choke. You should also
   consider getting an ID tag, but this may not be necessary if the puppy
   has a registered microchip; ultimately, you simply want to make sure
   there's a way for him to be returned to you if he gets lost.

Photo Courtesy
of Elizabeth Lamborn

NOTE: Shelties have a lot of fluffy fur, especially around their necks, as well as little heads. It can be difficult to fit a collar around their neck that they can't slip off, without it being too tight. Winnie can easily slip out of her collar, so we have to put a harness on her whenever we go on walks. (However, she is fully aware of this fact and doesn't like having her freedom restricted, so she'll pout and act dramatic, pretending to be unable to walk, whenever we put her harness on her.)

5. **Leash:** Again, pretty standard. You can decide if you want a retractable leash, which will allow the puppy to roam farther, or if you prefer a more basic leash.

6. **Toys:** You'll want to get a combination of chew toys, toys for tug-of-war, and balls for fetch. Keep in mind that your Sheltie will develop his own personal preferences, and you may need to go through a little trial and error to figure out what he likes.

7. **Dog Crate:** As I said before, you will need to buy a dog crate that is big enough for your Sheltie to comfortably stand and turn around in, but it should be small enough to give him a feeling of security. You can either size up as your puppy grows or buy one that has an adjustable divider.

8. **Dog Bed**: The softer and comfier, the better. Remember, you will need bedding to put inside the dog crate, as well as possibly a separate bed to give an alternative option for napping.

9. **Puppy Gate / Play Pen**: This item is optional. If you are planning to section off a designated puppy-safe area in your home, you will want to have any necessary gates set up ahead of time.

10. **Carpet Cleaner:** You will need to buy an odor-eliminating enzyme cleaner designed for pets. This item is NOT optional. Trust me on this one—you're going to need it!

Other essentials you will need to buy in the beginning but don't necessarily have to have before you bring your puppy home (although I would highly encourage it) include grooming supplies—brush, nail clippers, puppy shampoo, and toothbrush/toothpaste—treats, and poop bags (although plastic grocery bags make a cheaper alternative and are just as effective). You should also talk to your vet about getting flea and tick prevention, as well as heartworm medication.

Bringing Your Sheltie Home

When you pick up your Sheltie from the breeder or shelter, make sure you also pick up any necessary paperwork and ask about the puppy's current feeding schedule. You'll need to bring a second person with you who can hold the puppy in the car, as well as a blanket and something for the puppy to chew on. If bringing a second person with you is not possible, you can bring a crate. However, this will likely scare the puppy, especially if he is not crate-trained yet. Before leaving, you should give the puppy ample opportunity to relieve himself.

You can encourage the puppy to get in the car by giving him a treat and letting him explore a little. You want the puppy to be as comfortable as possible; if the first car ride is traumatic, this will make a lasting impression on his mind. However, you absolutely cannot let the puppy roam free while you are driving, as this can endanger both you and the puppy, so this is where the second person comes in. Since airbags are dangerous for puppies, this person should sit in the backseat to hold the puppy and try to comfort him. The air in the car should be comfortably warm and well ventilated. The puppy will likely cry, but the person holding him can pet him and try to distract him with the chew toy. It can also be helpful if the blanket has a familiar scent, so the puppy can feel more at home while wrapped or resting on it.

If bringing a second person is not a possibility, you can line a crate with soft blankets and put a chew toy inside. Encourage the puppy to climb into the crate by tempting him with a treat and waiting for him to go in willingly; you should not force or shove him inside. Make sure the crate is completely secure inside the car, so it does not move around if you have to stop suddenly. Still, even with all this preparation, the puppy will most likely cry and be scared, which may cause adverse feelings toward both the crate and the car in the future. I strongly advise you to wait to pick up the puppy until you can bring a second person with you.

Depending on how far away you live, you will likely have to make at least one stop on the way home. Puppies can generally hold their bladders for the number of hours corresponding to the number of months in age, so a two-month-old puppy can hold it for up to two hours; however, the stress of the car ride may decrease this number. If the puppy has not yet been properly vaccinated, you will need to avoid highway rest stops and areas with designated doggy areas since the bacteria in other dogs' urine or feces can infect your puppy.

*Photo Courtesy
of Julia Scharding*

Introducing Your Sheltie to Your Other Pets

"Some Shelties self appoint themselves to 'middle manager' positions where they scold other pets for breaking your rules. This is usually in the form of barking at a cat that's scratching furniture or oddly barking at another dog that was told to stop barking."

LINNEA GULSTAD
Sunny Shelties

If you already have pets living in your house, adding a new puppy to the mix can be disruptive to their lives as well. While there will likely be some tension at first, there are some steps you can take to make the transition as smooth as possible; still, you will have to be patient and understand that it will likely take time before your fur babies get along.

Introducing to Your Cat. If you own a cat, you will need to move her food, water, and litter box to an area where the new puppy cannot mess with them. After all, your cat would probably not appreciate having someone else eat her food, and you definitely don't want to end up finding the puppy digging in the litter box or eating the cat's poop. You should move these items before bringing the puppy home, so your cat can have time to adjust to the new arrangement without having to simultaneously deal with the stress of having a puppy in the house. You should also make sure your cat has places she can retreat to where the puppy cannot reach her, such as a cat tower or windowsill, in order to give her a safe haven away from prying puppy noses.

Before introducing your Sheltie to your cat, you should take the puppy on a long walk or play with him to get out some of his energy. While he will likely still be on high alert when meeting the cat, this should help him be at least a little calmer. You need to understand that Shelties are herding dogs, so your Sheltie will likely try to prevent your cat from moving and chase after her if she runs.

When Winnie met my cat Mele (short for Mele Kalikimaka, which is Hawaiian for "Merry Christmas"), Mele pulled a muscle trying to run away and ended up limping for quite a while afterwards. This is a risk to be aware of, especially with older cats. While it is typically best to let the animals interact with each other naturally and only interfere if necessary, you may need to hold your Sheltie back to prevent him from chasing your cat. Your Sheltie will likely be excited and curious, but your cat might be terrified; therefore, you should give your cat the chance to escape and observe from a safe distance. Eventually, both will calm down and learn to at least tolerate each other, if not like each other.

Introducing to Your Dog. If you already have a dog in the house, the relationship may be more complicated. Your current dog will likely be territorial of his home, so before bringing home the new puppy, you should put away any favorite toys or possessions, such as a bed. You will also need to introduce the dogs on neutral grounds, not in your home or yard. Many breeders and shelters have a designated room or fenced-in area where you can bring your dog to meet the puppy, or you can ask to meet in a park or another third-party location. This will help the initial meeting go much more smoothly, especially if your current dog is already well

Photo Courtesy of Nicole Zaffuto

socialized. It can also be helpful if you take the two dogs on a walk together, with each leash being held by a different person, so they can get used to being around each other. However, this may not be possible if the puppy has not received the necessary vaccinations yet, so you should first check with the breeder.

When you bring the puppy home, you should give him a chance to explore his new surroundings before introducing your other dog into the equation. Once you bring your current dog back into the room, he will likely become more on guard than when they met before, but the transition should be easier if he is already at least semi-familiar with the puppy. You should not be surprised if your dog growls or snaps at the puppy, though, as he establishes this is his home and he's the alpha. Your dog may also become annoyed at the puppy's antics, such as jumping on him when he's sleeping, and will growl or pin him down to teach him better manners. All of this is completely normal and appropriate behavior. You should not interfere unless there's a legitimate concern that one of the dogs will hurt the other, or if you find that your dog is aggressively bullying the puppy.

It will take time for the dogs to get used to each other and for the puppy to learn how to properly interact with the older dog. Eventually, things will calm down, though, and your dog may even welcome having a new playmate. Still, with both your children and your current pets, you should not leave them alone together until you are completely comfortable knowing they will interact nicely and no one will get hurt. This may take a few weeks. Until then, you will need to keep your puppy in a separate room or put him in his kennel when you are unable to supervise.

When Peace is not Possible. Ultimately, the goal is for everyone living in your house to be friends and live harmoniously. However, what happens if this is not the case? If several weeks pass and the animals are still excessively stressed or aggressive towards one another, you may have a problem. Before taking any drastic steps, you should talk to your vet or dog trainer and ask for advice on how to best alleviate the problem.

However, if you follow all the appropriate steps and still do not see any improvement, you may have to consider giving the puppy back to the breeder or rescue. Personally, in these situations, I am a strong believer that you should remain loyal to your older dog. After all, this is his home, and you have been his family for all these years; I do not believe you should give him away to replace him with a puppy. Still, it is not an easy decision, and it's one that should be made only as an absolute last resort. The hope is that you will be able to figure out a solution that will work well for everyone, so your household can be peaceful and happy once again.

The First Night Home

"They will bark and cry if left in a crate or different room. Do not engage, yell to them, or return until they have been quiet for a while. They will quickly learn to sleep through the night quietly."

LINNEA GULSTAD
Sunny Shelties

The first day home can be exciting and overwhelming for both you and your puppy. You should try to keep the first day as quiet and relaxed as possible. Your Sheltie will need time to adapt to his new environment, investigate all the new smells, and take lots of naps. You can expect your puppy to sleep a lot, and he will likely need to go outside as soon as he wakes up. In general, you should plan to take your puppy outside at least every hour, if not more. While there will still be accidents, it's best to begin potty training as soon as possible and establish a routine for you and your puppy.

You can also expect the first night to not be very restful. After all, this is a scary time for your puppy; it's likely the first night he's ever spent away from his mother and siblings. Your puppy should sleep in his kennel—which again should be lined with soft bedding—either in the puppy-designated area or in your bedroom, depending on your preference.

When my husband and his sisters each got their own puppy, the puppy stayed near the kitchen, but the respective owner slept on the floor in front of the kennel, which helped comfort the puppy and strengthen their bond. (Though the first night my husband had Winnie, he quickly took her out of the kennel and let her sleep on his chest!)

You will need to take the puppy outside several times during the night, but during these times, you should minimize the amount of attention you give him. He needs to

SHELTIES IN BOOKS
River Love

River Love: The True Story of a Wayward Sheltie, a Woman, and a Magical Place Called Rivershire by Tricia Frey is a memoir about Tricia and her experience purchasing a river property in 2005. A few months after purchasing the property, Tricia found a skittish Sheltie that she named Sheldon. This book is a story of "resilience, healing, redemption, and—most of all— love." This book was published in 2020 by Mission Point Press.

Photo Courtesy
of Raymond Ong

learn that nighttime is a time for sleep, and if you play with him and pet him every time he cries, this habit will continue.

Still, your puppy will cry at least throughout the first night, but there are a few tricks you can try to help comfort your puppy and give him a sense of security:

1. Ask the breeder ahead of time if you can take home a piece of bedding. You can put this in your puppy's kennel, so it has a familiar smell and feels more like home. If this isn't possible, you can also bring an old t-shirt, towel, or something similar to rub on the puppy's mother to make it smell like her.

2. Give the puppy a friend. Put a stuffed animal of similar size in the kennel with him, so he feels less alone. This will allow him to snuggle up

against it as if it's one of his littermates. If possible, it can be helpful to bring this item to the breeder as well and rub it on the puppy's litter-mates, so it holds their scent.

3. Hide an analog clock in the puppy's bedding. The ticking will mimic the sound of the mother's heartbeat. Nowadays, you can also find a stuffed animal specifically designed to make steady heartbeat sounds, and some even have a heating pad built in.

4. Some people also heat up a sock full of rice or a hot water bottle, so the puppy can have something warm to cuddle with, which will remind him of the warmth of his mother and siblings.

You probably won't get much rest the first night—or possibly several nights—but don't worry, it will get better. It will simply take some time for your puppy to get comfortable with his new surroundings and become used to the new routine. After all, it's a big, scary world out there for a little puppy! Now, it's your job to be his safe place and provide a sense of secu-rity and love.

CHAPTER FIVE
Housetraining

"A dog should never be unattended in the house until fully housebroken. This means on leash, directly supervised in a small room, or safely in a crate."

LINNEA GULSTAD
Sunny Shelties

Housetraining can be one of the most overwhelming parts of getting a new puppy. Everyone wants to focus on how adorable and silly the puppy is and how much fun he is to play with, but no one wants to think about stepping in puddles of urine or finding droppings around

Photo Courtesy of Catrina Mehltretter

the house; however, unfortunately, it's a package deal. Therefore, you want to figure out how to get past the bathroom-accident phase as quickly and painlessly as possible, so you can focus on all the positive qualities of your little fluff ball instead.

The key is consistency. You need to establish a routine early on and stick with it. Your puppy will need to go outside immediately after you wake up, and I mean immediately—don't lie in bed scrolling through Instagram or stop to brush your teeth first—as well as right before you go to bed and several other times throughout the day.

Puppies generally eat three to four small meals a day, so you'll need to come up with a regular feeding schedule, which will then influence when your puppy needs to go outside. Puppies have extremely small bladders, so you should keep an eye on when your puppy eats and drinks and take him outside soon afterwards. Other times he will likely need to go outside are when he wakes up from a nap or when he's done playing or chewing on a toy. When you see signs such as sniffing the ground, circling, or general restlessness, you'll need to quickly head outside. Overall, you're going to end up making a lot of trips outside with your puppy on a daily basis.

Even if you have a fully fenced-in yard, you should not allow your puppy outside on his own quite yet. You first need to establish trust, make sure your puppy is familiar and comfortable with his environment, and be confident he is actually doing his business when he is supposed to.

To start with, you will need to take him outside on the leash and create an established "potty" area where your puppy knows he is supposed to relieve himself. When he successfully goes potty in this area, wait until he's done, then shower him with praise and give him a treat right away; do not wait until you get back inside because he needs to understand the connection between the action and the reward. You also should not play with him outside until he's done with his business, or he'll get distracted and forget he needs to go.

To minimize the need to take your puppy outside during the night, you should pick up the water bowl around two and a half hours before going to bed. This will allow the puppy time to digest any excess water remaining in his system without introducing new water that will need to be expelled after you've gone to bed. Your puppy will likely still cry to go outside during the night, at least to start with, but hopefully not as often. When you take the puppy outside during the night, do not play with him or give him attention other than rewarding him for relieving himself outside. You do not want your puppy to think that it's time to play and start waking you up simply because he wants attention. Your puppy needs to understand that night is a time for sleep.

Crate Training

"I'm a strong advocate of crate training. Always ask if they need to go outside. Use a word or phrase every time you go out with them such as Go Potty, Do Hurry Up, Do your Duty...etc. PRAISE, PRAISE, PRAISE when they go to the bathroom. They catch on really fast. Watch for them to get restless and start sniffing around and sometimes whine...It usually means it is time to go out. Always take them out whenever they wake up, after eating or playing for a period of time."

SUZI BEACHAM
Shalamar Shelties

Whenever you are not able to directly supervise your puppy, you should put him in his crate, so you know he is in a safe, secure place where he won't get into any trouble. This will also be where he sleeps at night, at least to start with.

Photo Courtesy of Jennifer Lavers

Here are the basic steps for crate training your puppy, based on the recommendations from the Humane Society of America[1]:

1. When introducing your Sheltie to his crate, you should try to create positive associations with the location. Do not force him inside, but rather encourage him and let him explore it willingly. If your Sheltie hesitates to go in or near the crate, you can try placing a treat just outside the door of the crate, then towards the front of it, then all the way in the back. When your puppy does go inside, be sure to give him lots of praise and affirmation.

2. You should feed your Sheltie meals inside the crate, so he forms positive associations with being inside it. If he's still hesitant to go all the way in, you can start by putting the bowl as far inside as he will go without being stressed and slowly push it back each time you feed him. Once he is comfortable eating all the way inside the crate, you can start to close the door. To start with, you should let him back out as soon as he's done eating, but you can slowly increase the time he is left inside the crate until he stays inside for ten minutes after meals. You can also introduce a specific command, such as Crate or Kennel, whenever your puppy goes into the crate for mealtime, so he knows what to expect. To this day, Winnie eats all her meals inside her crate; all we have to do is say "Kennel," and she'll happily go inside and wait to be fed.

3. Practice leaving your puppy alone in the crate. Once your Sheltie is comfortable with being in the crate, you can have him go inside it by saying the corresponding command, then praise him when he obeys. Close the door and sit next to it quietly for a few minutes, without interacting with the puppy, then get up and go into another room for a few minutes. Come back, sit quietly again, then let the puppy out. Repeat this process several times a day, gradually increasing the amount of time the puppy is in the crate and the amount of time you're out of the room.

4. Once your Sheltie can stay in the crate for at least thirty minutes without becoming overly anxious, you can start to leave him in the crate when you leave the house. You can praise him when he goes in the crate, but you should keep your departures and arrivals as quiet and unemotional as possible to avoid any excess excitement or anxiety regarding the process. To start with, you should not be gone long; remember that puppies have small bladders and will need to go outside. You should also continue having your Sheltie go into the crate at other times throughout the day, so he does not solely associate it with you leaving.

---

1   https://www.humanesociety.org/resources/crate-training-101

Here are a few additional tips to consider when crate-training your puppy:

1. NEVER use the crate as a punishment. It is meant to be a place where your Sheltie can go to feel safe and comforted, not a penalty box.

2. Make the crate cozy. Shelties enjoy snuggling up in soft blankets, so putting a bed and/or blanket in the crate can make it more comfortable and inviting. You might also want to consider putting in a small chew toy, so your Sheltie can keep himself occupied while you're away.

3. Keep the mood relaxed. When first acclimating your puppy to the crate, do not try to get him to go inside when he's super energetic and playful. Wait until he calms down, so he associates the crate with being quiet and relaxed. You might even find that your Sheltie starts napping in his crate voluntarily.

4. Your puppy will likely cry, especially at first. The trick will be learning how to distinguish the cries indicating it's time to go outside from the whining saying he wants to play. If he starts to cry immediately after you put him in the crate, he's most likely simply protesting being left alone. If you take him out every time he whines, he will learn to cry whenever he wants to get out. However, if it's been a while since your puppy has gone outside, or if he recently ate or drank anything, you should take him outside. It's better to be safe than sorry.

The crate can also be an effective tool in housetraining your puppy. This is where it is important to make sure the crate you buy is not too big for your Sheltie. Your puppy will naturally hesitate to create a mess where he sleeps; however, if there is enough room, he will use the corner as a bathroom then simply sleep on the other side. You can put your puppy in the crate when it's nearing the time when he usually needs to go outside to help prevent any accidents.

When your puppy is in the crate, he will start to whimper and cry when he needs to go outside, which means he will start to recognize the bodily signals telling him it's time to go. When this happens, you will need to take him outside immediately. For a very young puppy, it can also be a good idea to pick him up and carry him outside to prevent him from stopping to pee on the way to the door. If the puppy doesn't successfully go potty when you take him outside, you can put him back in the crate then try again in a little while. Do not let him play outside of his crate until he has completed his business.

Play Pens and Puppy Pads

As we've already discussed, it can be a good idea to set up a play pen or gate to section off an area of your house where the puppy can play and sleep freely without getting into trouble. The puppy should have access to his crate as well as his toys and water bowl.

Ideally, this area should not have any carpets or rugs, so when the puppy does have an accident, the cleanup is easier. Some people also suggest using puppy pads, so the puppy has a designated place indoors where he can relieve himself if you are not able to immediately take him outside. Using a puppy pad helps to minimize cleanup and has the eventual goal of transitioning to only going outside once the puppy has stronger bladder control.

While some people find this method helpful, it can also make housetraining harder in the long run since it reinforces the idea that it is acceptable for the puppy to do his business inside the house. Your puppy will not automatically know how to use these pads, so you will need to train him by rewarding him whenever he relieves himself on the pad. Weaning the puppy off these pads can be difficult because once the pads are removed, the puppy will simply continue to go in that same spot. After all, he doesn't understand the difference between a pad and the floor. You might as well dedicate the time to train him to go outside from the very beginning, so the rules are straightforward and consistent.

Photo Courtesy
of Britt Mertens

When Accidents Happen

Even if you do everything right, and it feels like you're taking your puppy outside around the clock, accidents are bound to happen. Your puppy might get excited and not be able to contain himself, or you might turn your back for two seconds and miss the all-important signal. Either way, it's no one's fault. Your Sheltie is just a baby right now. He's still learning, and he's doing the best he can...and so are you.

If you catch your puppy in the act of soiling your floor or starting to squat, don't punish him. Interrupt him, scoop him up, and take him outside. If he finishes outside, give him lots of praise.

If you find an unwelcome surprise on the floor after the fact, there isn't anything you can do except clean it up. There is no point in punishing the puppy at this point; he won't understand what he did wrong and will just become afraid of you. He may even start avoiding relieving himself in your presence altogether, which is the opposite of what you want. And whatever you do, do NOT rub your puppy's nose in the mess. It will only make more of a mess for you to clean up, your puppy will be scared and confused, and it's just plain disgusting.

When you clean up an accident, it is crucial that you use an odor-eliminating enzyme cleaner designed for pets. If your puppy can still smell the area where the accident occurred, he will continue to do his business in that spot. If you find that your puppy is constantly having accidents in the same place, it likely means that you are not cleaning it up properly, and you might want to consider getting a different cleaning product.

Leaving Your Puppy Home Alone

Most people aren't able to stay home 24/7. Whether you're going to work, running an errand, or going out with a friend, you'll need to leave your puppy home alone at some point. When you do, your puppy will need to stay in his crate. Even if he's been getting the hang of potty training, you don't want to make the mistake of giving him the run of the house too early. While he will eventually graduate to staying in the gated-off puppy space, keeping him in the crate will be the best way to prevent accidents while you're gone.

Still, even if your puppy is in his crate, he can't hold it forever. The general rule of thumb is that a puppy is capable of holding his bladder for the number of hours corresponding to the number of months in age, up until eight or nine months. For example, a three-month-old puppy can hold it for up to three hours. If given no other option, the puppy will soil his crate, which can then become a difficult habit to break.

If you are going to be gone for an extended period of time, you will need to make arrangements for someone to come and let the puppy outside throughout the day, such as a relative, neighbor, or professional pet-sitter. This person will also need to be aware of your puppy's feeding schedule and provide meals as necessary. The routine should remain as consistent as possible to avoid confusing your puppy. Still, keep in mind that puppies should not be left home alone all day in general. They need to spend time playing and bonding with you in addition to going outside. If you're going to be gone all day, every day, and aren't able to be home with your Sheltie, it might not be the best time to get a puppy.

Photo Courtesy
of Rebecca Loyd

Main Takeaways

"The last thing to do at night is to take them outside to potty. Be sure to praise them or give them a tiny treat reward when they do their business. You will learn whether they are more food or praise motivated. Remember, they are young & can only hold their bladder for short periods of time. If they are napping, just before they wake up, pick them up & carry them outside to potty. Then praise & reward them."

SHERRY DEEDS
BellaRose Shelties

Photo Courtesy
of Kelsey Gordon

The first few weeks with a new puppy are exciting, but they also involve a lot of time and effort, especially when housetraining. This effort will be worthwhile in the long run, but in the meantime, it can be exhausting and frustrating. There is no definitive time frame of when your puppy will be perfectly housetrained; it's different for every puppy.

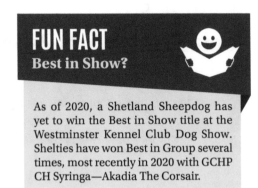

FUN FACT
Best in Show?

As of 2020, a Shetland Sheepdog has yet to win the Best in Show title at the Westminster Kennel Club Dog Show. Shelties have won Best in Group several times, most recently in 2020 with GCHP CH Syringa—Akadia The Corsair.

However, it will eventually click, and your Sheltie's intelligence and intuition should help the process progress faster than it would for some breeds.

These initial weeks will involve many trips outdoors, as well as many accidents. Just remember:

1. **Consistency is key.** Create a designated "potty" area where your puppy knows he is supposed to go. Establish a schedule and stick to it.

2. **Generously reward correct behavior.** Praise your puppy and give a treat immediately after your puppy relieves himself outside, so your puppy understands what he is being rewarded for.

3. **Do not punish accidents.** Punishment will do more harm than good in this scenario.

4. **Carefully clean up accidents.** Make sure no trace remains, including smell, or else your puppy will continue to go in the same spot.

5. **Use the crate to your advantage.** Crate your puppy when you are unable to properly supervise, and use the crate as a tool to help prevent accidents and to teach your puppy to recognize his bodily signals when it is time to go.

6. **Try to be patient.** Your Sheltie wants to please you; he simply needs time to learn and grow.

CHAPTER SIX
Socializing With People And Animals

"Although they adapt to any age of owner, they do need to be exposed to a variety of people/children when they are still puppies in order to keep their naturally shy nature from being predominant."

VIOLET EARL
Earl's Dogpatch

Photo Courtesy of Marilyn O'Donnell

Proper socialization is an essential part of raising any puppy, but it is arguably even more important when raising a Shetland Sheepdog. Due to their reserved nature, Shelties are prone to becoming overly skittish toward people and other animals unless they become accustomed to meeting strangers as a young puppy. According to the AKC, the first three months of a puppy's life are a vital socialization window, which will shape the puppy's personality and the way he reacts to his environment for the rest of his life. This is where going to a responsible breeder can also be helpful, for this socialization process should start even before the puppy is transferred into your care.

SHELTIES ON TV
Mickey's Farm

Mickey the Sheepdog is the star of the Canadian children's television show *Mickey's Farm*. Alongside his costar Megan, Mickey the Sheltie lives on a farm and loves adventure. Mikey is voiced by Peter MacDonald in the first two seasons and Erin Mackey in seasons 3 through 5. The show is produced by Best Boy Entertainment and is geared towards preschoolers and young children.

This is an area where I wish we had done a better job when Winnie was a young puppy. While she grew familiar with my husband's immediate family and their dogs, she was never properly exposed to people or dogs outside of the family. This lack of socialization played a major role in shaping her personality, and even today she is extremely wary toward strangers, which results in a lot of barking as well as fear when being petted. She eventually calms down, especially if we exhibit trust toward the new people, but in general, she tends to be extremely shy and nervous. If we could go back in time, we would make more of an effort to expose her to new places, people, and animals earlier in her development.

It is important to note, however, that even with proper socialization, Shelties will maintain a certain level of caution when meeting a stranger, and this reserve is listed as part of the breed standard. While there are always exceptions, Shelties are generally not the type of dog that will run up to greet new people or animals. They tend to hang back, carefully observing the stranger's behavior as well as their master's response to the stranger, before deciding if they're comfortable approaching or being petted. The goal of socialization is not to remove this natural reserve, but rather to prevent this reserve from developing into excessive shyness or fear. A well-socialized Sheltie will wait, assess the situation, then become outgoing and friendly once the situation is deemed safe.

Meeting New People

Finding people to socialize your puppy with shouldn't be too hard; after all, once your friends and family members hear you have a new puppy, they'll likely be dying to come visit. You can start by hosting a small gathering, either at your house or a friend's house, and inviting a variety of people. You don't want to overwhelm your puppy by having a swarm of people surround him all at once, so you should introduce the puppy in groups of two to three people. This will give your puppy time to grow accustomed to all the new smells and voices.

When introducing your Sheltie to someone new, it is important to remind the person to be patient and allow the Sheltie to make the first move. As we've already discussed, your Sheltie will need a moment to judge whether the situation is safe before approaching, and if a stranger suddenly lunges toward him, the Sheltie will likely become more on guard. The new people can crouch down and offer their hand to sniff, allowing the Sheltie to approach and become comfortable before they try to pet the puppy.

Once your puppy has received any necessary vaccinations and you have the go-ahead from your vet, you can take your puppy out of his comfort zone

Photo Courtesy of Andrea Porter

and introduce him to new places, such as other neighborhoods, parks, and the pet store. The whole world is new to your puppy, so you want to expose him to as many new environments and people as possible. The AKC suggests making a game out of it, such as a scavenger hunt, and trying to introduce your puppy to people of all shapes, sizes, and races; people wearing hats, hoodies, or sunglasses; people in a wheelchair or using crutches; people running, skipping, or walking with a limp...as much variety as you can find, so your puppy is exposed to all sorts of people, not one specific group.

In a similar manner, your puppy should be exposed to as many different places, walking surfaces, sounds, and objects as possible. This will allow your puppy to grow into a well-rounded adult who won't be afraid when encountering something new and unfamiliar. As you explore, make sure you give your puppy plenty of affirmation through treats and praise, so your puppy will form positive associations with being out in public and interacting with people.

Shelties and Children

Introducing your Sheltie to children can be trickier than introducing him to adults since children can be more unpredictable. As we discussed earlier, Shelties are extremely gentle, and it is highly unlikely that a Sheltie would ever intentionally hurt a child. However, Shelties are also very sensitive and tend to be nervous, so if a child is too rough or chases them, they will learn to fear and avoid children. Once again, early exposure will be helpful because if a puppy is used to being around children from an early age, he will be less likely to have any issues with children as he grows into an adult dog.

It is important that any children who interact with the Sheltie behave properly, so the Sheltie does not develop any negative associations with children. You will need to remind any children who want to pet your Sheltie to wait for the puppy to approach them and to be very gentle when petting the puppy. The children also need to understand that they should never chase the puppy, even if they just want to play with him, since that will scare the puppy.

This is another issue we've encountered with Winnie. When our nieces and nephews became toddlers, they started chasing Winnie, even though they were told not to. Now Winnie tends to nervously avoid them, and she is usually scared of any other children we encounter and will back away if they try to pet her. If she had been properly socialized with children as a puppy, her reaction may have been less extreme.

Socializing with Other Dogs

"Be sure your puppy has its vaccinations before taking it out in public. Once your puppy has had them, then it's time to meet other dogs under controlled circumstances. The nice thing about Shelties is they are easy to pick up. Be aware of dog body language so that you can prevent a meet and greet from turning into a confrontation."

LAURA WILLSON
Wildwest Shelties

Photo Courtesy of Shari King

Photo Courtesy
of Kaiu Guk

Proper socialization with other dogs is just as important as socialization with humans. After all, whether you're walking your Sheltie around your neighborhood, the park, or a hiking trail, you're bound to encounter other dogs, and you want to make sure the interaction goes as smoothly as possible.

Once your puppy has received any necessary vaccinations and your vet deems it safe, you can start to introduce your Sheltie to other dogs. If you have a friend or relative with a dog, you can organize a puppy playdate. This can be a good way to start socializing your puppy since you can be assured of the other dog's temperament, and the dogs can have time to get used to interacting with each other, rather than a passing interaction on the street. It can also be a good idea to invite your friends to bring their dogs over to your house, so your Sheltie can become used to other dogs being in his space. Shelties can be very territorial, so this can become an issue if they are not acclimated early to the idea of having other dogs in and near their home.

When encountering another dog on the street, always ask the owner's permission before allowing the dogs to interact. After all, you don't know how the other dog will respond, and even if the other dog is friendly, he might not be up-to-date on his vaccinations, or the owner might not have the time or desire to stop, which you need to respect as well.

Another good place to socialize your Sheltie with other puppies is in a puppy obedience class. These classes provide a good opportunity for your Sheltie to interact with other puppies and learn to follow your commands, even with the distraction of other puppies nearby.

68

Interactions with Other Animals

When introducing your Sheltie to a cat, make sure the cat has a method of escape, such as a windowsill or ledge, and be prepared to hold back your puppy if necessary. Your Sheltie may try to chase and "herd" the cat, or he might be scared of the cat. Never leave your Sheltie alone with the cat unsupervised unless you are completely confident in both animals' behavior. It is highly unlikely that the Sheltie would hurt the cat, but the cat might scratch the puppy in self-defense, which can cause considerable damage, especially if the puppy is scratched in the eye.

Interactions with other household pets should be determined on a case-by-case basis. Small animals, such as hamsters and gerbils, should not be allowed to play with the puppy. The Sheltie would not intentionally try to hurt them, but accidents do happen. Winnie once accidentally killed a mouse by bopping it on the head to keep it from moving, then was distraught when she realized it was dead.

Bigger animals might be safer, but you will still need to carefully supervise, for the Sheltie's safety as well as the other animal. We took care of a

Photo Courtesy
of Catrina Mehltretter

baby ferret for a while and tried to get her to play with Winnie. The ferret kept nipping at Winnie's paws and trying to climb her fur. Winnie didn't do anything to defend herself; she just stood there looking sad and stressed out, so we had to separate them.

If you want to introduce your Sheltie to farm animals, you should not assume that just because Shelties were bred as herding dogs, they will automatically be comfortable interacting with livestock. You will need to allow your Sheltie time to explore the new environment, then introduce the puppy to the other animals slowly. First, allow the Sheltie to sniff the other animal through the fence and allow the other animal freedom to run away if desired. Once your Sheltie is comfortable with this, you can bring the Sheltie into the fenced area under careful supervision with one person handling the puppy and another person handling the other animal. Your Sheltie might be curious, or he might be terrified. Allow the puppy to sniff and explore the new animal as desired, but do not force the interaction.

When Winnie was a puppy, my husband tried to introduce her to some lambs, thinking it would be cute to see her try to herd the little lambs. Winnie immediately froze, petrified, and lay down in the middle of the pen while the lambs ran away from my husband and toward Winnie. It's a miracle none of them stepped on her. This is why it is important to introduce the animals gradually and under close supervision!

Understanding the Herding Instinct.

Shetland Sheepdogs were originally bred to herd the sheep and cattle in the Shetland Islands, and even today, their descendants are born with an innate drive to herd other animals. However, this does not mean your Sheltie will automatically understand how to round up sheep and bring them back to the barn; that will require specialized training. What it does mean is that your Sheltie will be automatically attracted to movement and feel the strong urge to prevent this movement. This urge results in chasing—such as when a bunny or squirrel runs across your yard—as well as attempts to prevent you or other household members, including children and pets, from leaving the room.

When Winnie was a puppy, my husband would stand in the kitchen while making himself lunch, and he constantly found himself trapped in corners as Winnie subtly nudged him along and blocked him in.

Understanding this instinct is an important part of understanding how your Sheltie will interact with other animals. Don't be surprised if your Sheltie tries to prevent your cat from walking around freely, or if he suddenly lunges after a squirrel when you're out on a walk—which is another important reminder to never trust a Sheltie off-leash. However, Shelties were bred to herd animals, not kill them, so they are usually extremely gentle and will not intentionally hurt another animal.

Is It Too Late?

Of course, properly socializing a puppy during the first three or four months of age is ideal, but what do you do if you miss this window or if you adopt an older dog? I can tell you from experience that trying to socialize an older dog, especially a Sheltie, will be much harder but not impossible. Many of the same principles of socialization apply, but you will need to take it slow to avoid stressing out your Sheltie. Shelties are very sensitive, and if they have already become overly shy and skittish around strangers, trying to force interaction will only increase their fear of social situations.

One of the best ways to get your Sheltie to trust someone new is to exhibit trust yourself. Shelties are highly attuned to tone and emotion, so you can show your Sheltie that he has nothing to fear by enthusiastically greeting the person and remaining calm throughout the interaction. It can also be helpful to instruct the other person to ignore the Sheltie until the Sheltie initiates the first interaction. If your Sheltie is still too afraid to approach, you can offer treats to lure the Sheltie closer. Once the Sheltie approaches and eventually allows the person to pet him, give him lots of praise and encouragement. You want to form as many positive associations with these interactions as possible.

Photo Courtesy of Jason Henry

Recently, we invited some friends to bring their new puppy to our apartment to meet Winnie. The puppy was very friendly, outgoing, and eager to play with Winnie, but Winnie was not thrilled about having a strange dog in her home. My sweet, gentle baby who's scared of her own shadow was suddenly aggressive, growling and baring her teeth. She wouldn't hurt the puppy, but she certainly let him know that he wasn't welcome. I was shocked; I had never seen her act like this before.

We tried taking the dogs on a walk to allow them to grow accustomed to each other, during which they both exhibited perfect behavior, but as soon as we got back to the apartment, Winnie became aggressive again. Her reaction likely would have been far less extreme if we had introduced the dogs on neutral ground.

Winnie is usually well mannered when we pass other dogs on a hiking trail—she'll bark from a distance, then sniff them when they approach or freeze while they sniff her—but any dogs in our neighborhood or near her home, she views as a threat.

To avoid this problem, you should introduce your Sheltie to other dogs at a neutral location, then invite your friends to bring their dog to your house once the dogs are comfortable with each other, so your Sheltie can get used to the idea of other dogs being in his space. When you invite another dog to your home, put any objects your Sheltie might be particularly possessive of, such as a bed or favorite toy, out of reach to prevent any fighting. Keep in mind that Shelties are naturally very territorial, so even proper socialization may not eliminate all issues with dogs being near or in your home. However, the goal is to acclimate your Sheltie to other dogs, minimizing any aggressive behavior, so they can eventually calm down and interact peacefully.

Overall, the answer is no, it is not too late. I won't lie to you—it will be much harder to socialize a Sheltie as an adult than as a puppy; however, it isn't impossible. We're still trying to rectify some of the mistakes that were made when Winnie was a puppy, but while it isn't always easy, she has made major progress. She is starting to get used to us having friends over to the apartment and will even be friendly toward some of our neighbors—after initially barking and alerting us to their presence, of course.

CHAPTER SEVEN
Physical And Mental Exercise

"They love a daily walk through the neighborhood or a nice run in the park. Let them sniff & explore. It's like reading the newspaper for us. It mentally stimulates their minds."

SHERRY DEEDS
BellaRose Shelties

Shelties are very high-energy dogs, so they require copious amounts of daily exercise to keep them happy and healthy. However, when trying to exercise your Sheltie, you need to understand that simply going on walks isn't going to be enough. Your Sheltie needs both physical and mental exercise, as well as different varieties within each category.

Photo Courtesy
of Nadine Shortland

Age-Appropriate Exercise

How much exercise a Sheltie needs depends on the age of the individual dog. Puppies generally get short bursts of energy where they will be super hyperactive for a brief period, then collapse and fall asleep. Puppies do not have good cardiovascular endurance, so you should not expect your puppy to be able to go on long walks or hikes just yet. Let your puppy be the guide, telling you when he's ready to play and when he needs a nap, and do not push him beyond his capabilities.

Over-exercising a puppy can cause long-term joint and bone problems. When playing with your puppy, you need to keep in mind that a puppy's bone structure is not fully developed at this stage, so what might result in a sprain or pulled muscle in an adult dog could cause considerable damage for a puppy. To help your puppy stay safe, you should start with short walks, then gradually increase the length as the puppy ages. Also, when playing tug-of-war, you need to keep the toy low to avoid straining your puppy's neck.

Your Sheltie's endurance will increase as he ages. Older puppies and young adult Shelties have boundless energy, which can be difficult to keep up with. At this stage, your Sheltie will require longer walks and play sessions several times a day. If you're gone during the day, you will need to exercise your Sheltie in the morning before you leave, when you get home, and before you go to bed, in addition to possibly finding someone to exercise your Sheltie during the day, depending on how long you will be gone. Keep in mind that Shelties do not share the same sleep schedule as humans—they typically take sporadic naps throughout the day rather than having a single deep sleep at night—so do not be surprised if your Sheltie has a sudden burst of energy in the evening when you're trying to wind down for bedtime.

Older dogs are typically more willing to lounge around during the day, but even at this stage, your Sheltie will need exercise to keep him healthy, happy, and in shape. Too sedentary of a lifestyle can cause your Sheltie to feel the effects of age more severely and can increase the risk of obesity. We will discuss age-appropriate exercise for senior dogs more in the final chapter.

Types of Physical Exercise

Remember when you were a child, you would always want dessert even though you claimed to be too full to finish dinner? You would tell your parents that your "dessert belly" was empty, even though your "dinner belly" was full. That's how it is with Shelties and exercise.

We can get home from a nice long walk with Winnie, expecting her to be exhausted, and she'll immediately beg to play. When trying to satiate your Sheltie's seemingly endless energy, you need to keep in mind his "appetite" for different types of exercise and incorporate a good variety into your daily routine.

CARDIO EXERCISES

Of course, you can always walk around your neighborhood, which is an easy and effective way to burn off some energy. Your Sheltie will also likely enjoy being able to patrol his territory and make sure everything is in good order...although he might not understand that your neighbor's dog is allowed to be at your neighbor's house! If you have more time, you can also switch things up by driving to a nearby park or even simply venturing into a different neighborhood, which will give your Sheltie the chance to explore.

Shelties can also be excellent hiking companions. Due to their natural agility, Shelties are able to bound up rocks and jump over logs, which is a great workout and provides excellent stimulation. However, make sure your Sheltie isn't taking on too big of an obstacle, and be ready to carry him if the terrain gets too difficult. Also, remember that while they are strong, Shelties are still little dogs, so you will need to take your Sheltie's level of endurance into consideration when planning the length of the hike; otherwise, you may end up carrying the dog the entire way back to your car. Still, you can always take breaks along the way to allow your Sheltie time to recharge. Also, don't forget to bring water to keep your Sheltie hydrated. We like to bring a collapsible water dish designed for hiking with dogs, which hooks onto the leash.

Running or jogging with your Sheltie can also be a good option, but this will depend on your Sheltie's disposition. Some shepherd dogs aren't good running companions because they will try to "herd" you.

I haven't experienced any difficulties in this area with Winnie, but when my family owned an Australian Cattle Dog mix named Penny, she would always heavily push into me when I tried to run or ride my bike with her. (I also still have a scar on my hip from being dragged down the road by Penny when my brother took off running, and I was left holding the leash while Penny bolted after him to round him back up... but thankfully, Shelties aren't strong enough to do that!)

You can always try going for a jog with your Sheltie and see how he responds. Depending on how strong your Sheltie's herding instinct is, he may enjoy it, or he may try to keep you in line by leaning into you, circling you, or lightly nipping at your heels.

 **PLAY TIME**

Playing with your Sheltie not only provides good exercise, but it also allows you to bond with your Sheltie. Seeing the excited look of "Really? We're doing this? You're gonna play with me?" is just as much of a reward as ensuring your Sheltie's physical wellbeing. The toy aisle in the pet store provides plenty of options for playing with your Sheltie, but you can also be creative by playing games such as hide-and-seek, where you run and hide, then call your puppy to come find you and shower him with praise when he succeeds.

Photo Courtesy of Gaby Garcia

When you play tug-of-war, you will need to be gentle. Shelties have sensitive mouths, so if you play roughly, it can cause their gums to bleed. If you notice any blood on the toy, simply stop the game and be more careful next time. Still, tug-of-war can be an enjoyable game for you both.

Winnie loves it; whenever she wins, she'll bring the toy back and wait for us to readjust our grip on it before starting again. If she's the one who's accidently too rough, and we say, "Ow," she'll also stop to come over and sniff or lick our hand to make sure we're alright before continuing the game.

Still, fetch is by far Winnie's favorite game. She was never properly taught how to play; she just watched my sister-in-law's dog Charlie play, then copied her. (Charlie was also blind, and even as a puppy, Winnie ended up becoming her eyes and would run with her and help her find the ball. Yes, we do have the sweetest dog in the world!) Winnie also never had any trouble giving the ball back; she even started putting the ball directly in my husband's hand completely unprompted.

Although not all dogs pick up on fetch as naturally as Winnie did, Shelties' herding instinct generally prompts them to run after movement, so having your Sheltie chase after a tennis ball shouldn't be a problem. If your Sheltie has trouble giving the ball back to you, you can encourage him with a treat until he gets the hang of the game. Fetch is a wonderful way to combine play and exercise without requiring much effort on your part.

The Importance of Job-Oriented Tasks. Shelties were bred to be working dogs, so they naturally crave having a job to do. Winnie's "job" is fetching the tennis ball, and she takes this task very seriously. Some people train their dogs to pick up their toys and put them in a basket. Others harness their dogs' herding instinct by playing a game called Treibball (pronounced Tribe-ball), where they train the Shelties or other herding dogs to "herd" exercise balls and push them into a designated goal. There are competitive leagues for this game, but you can also create your own version in your backyard. There are plenty of training videos online that can help you teach your Sheltie how to play.

No matter what avenue you choose, you need to give your Sheltie a designated job, so he can feel fulfilled. If your Sheltie is not given a job, he might invent one for himself, which you might not be too thrilled with!

Importance of Mental Exercise

"Shelties thrive in an environment that encourages learning. Active training of new tricks or refining current ones is one of the best ways to exercise a Sheltie's mind. This doesn't mean you need to teach fancy tricks, you can work on improving their 'stay', or performing sit or down at a distance, etc."

LINNEA GULSTAD
Sunny Shelties

In addition to providing physical exercise, you also need to exercise your Sheltie's brain. Shelties are extremely intellig`ent and will get bored easily unless they are given adequate stimulation. One way to provide mental exercise is through training. Training your Sheltie to listen to basic commands and perform tricks helps strengthen his mind in addition to making your life easier. You can also play games such as the shell game, where you invert three cups, put a treat under one of them, and let your Sheltie figure out where the treat is.

You can often accomplish two goals simultaneously. By playing interactive games with your Sheltie, you are stimulating his mind as well as exercising his body. The job-oriented tasks we just discussed are a great way to stimulate your Sheltie's mind and give him something to focus on.

You can also set up a makeshift agility course in your backyard. You don't have to invest in any fancy equipment—you can use an open

Photo Courtesy of Liana Maloney

cardboard box as a tunnel or have your Sheltie jump through a hula hoop or over a broom stick. If you find that you want to pursue agility further, you can order equipment online—such as a collapsible tunnel, adjustable jumps, and weave poles—or you can attend local classes and even start competing professionally.

Overall, the goal is to stimulate your Sheltie's mind. You don't have to do anything too fancy; try going for a walk in a new area and let your Sheltie sniff around and explore, or rotate out your Sheltie's toys so they become new and interesting again. This will help your Sheltie stay healthy and satisfied. After all, keeping your Sheltie's mind sharp is just as important as keeping his body strong.

Photo Courtesy of Kathy Allison

Tips for Keeping Your Sheltie Occupied

Despite your best efforts, you likely will not have enough free time to play as much as your Sheltie would like you to. Luckily for you, puppies, and even older dogs, take lots of naps, so you just have to figure out what to do during the times they are awake. Here are a few tips and tricks to keep your Sheltie occupied during the day:

1. **Go on walks, play, and interact with your Sheltie whenever you can.** If you work from home, you can use this as an opportunity to take a break from your work and get some fresh air; both you and your Sheltie will reap the benefits of this time together. If you are gone during the day, you will need to make plans for exercising your Sheltie while you're away, either by hiring a dog walker or enrolling your Sheltie in doggy daycare; however, don't let this completely replace your time interacting with your Sheltie yourself. Remember, in addition to fulfilling your Sheltie's physical needs, this time together is an opportunity to bond, and your Sheltie craves attention from you.

2. **Provide opportunities for solo play.** Chew toys can help keep your Sheltie occupied on his own. Keep in mind Shelties can be picky, so you might need to try a few different options before finding one your Sheltie likes. Winnie had a set of plastic keys to chew on when she was a puppy, and to this day, she refuses to touch any other type of chew toy. You can also try investing in a KONG ball and put peanut butter or canned pumpkin inside, and your Sheltie will stay busy trying to reach the yummy treat.

3. **Rotate toys.** Rotating between toys helps keep them from becoming boring by making them seem new and exciting all over again.

4. **Don't underestimate the utility of an ice cube.** Giving your Sheltie an ice cube is a great way to keep him cool, hydrated, and busy, especially during the hot summer months. If you want to add a special twist, you can also try freezing a treat or small toy inside the ice, so your Sheltie has further motivation to lick or chew through the block of ice.

5. **Provide background noise.** Some people suggest leaving the TV or radio on when you're out of the house, so your dog is not left alone in silence. Some dogs find this soothing and stimulating, while it doesn't make a difference for others. It could be worth experimenting with, especially if your Sheltie is experiencing separation anxiety.

6. **Provide access to a window.** Being able to see the outside world and watch what's going on can provide mental stimulation. (However, if there are people and/or dogs walking near your house, this might prompt some barking.)

7. **Consider giving your Sheltie a friend.** I understand that having two dogs can be a lot of work, and it isn't an option for everyone. However, if possible, having another dog in the house can be helpful, so the pups can play and keep each other entertained.

If you have a fully fenced-in backyard, you can also simply let your Sheltie outside to run around and chase squirrels to his heart's content. If you live in an apartment or don't have a fenced-in yard, you'll have to get more creative. It is possible to keep a Sheltie properly exercised even in a small space; you'll just need to take more walks, either in your neighborhood or a nearby park. Depending on the setup of your apartment, you can also play fetch indoors—just be careful to clear a path where nothing breakable is in the way. Shelties are small and often prefer small tennis balls, so the risk of mess is minimal. You also don't have to throw the ball very far, and you can even simply bounce the ball and let your Sheltie catch it rather than chase it. You can adapt any activity to the space available, and your Sheltie will be content.

Signs Your Sheltie is Bored

If your Sheltie does not get enough mental or physical exercise, his overall health and happiness will suffer, and he will likely exhibit consequent behaviors, indicating that you need to provide more stimulation. Here are some signs to watch for:

1. **Destructive behavior:** A clear sign that your Sheltie is not getting enough mental or physical exercise is if he starts getting into trouble. This can include getting into the trash, destroying furniture or other household objects, and digging up the garden in the backyard. After all, if you do not provide enough stimulation for him, your Sheltie will find ways to entertain himself.

2. **Excessive barking or whining:** If you are not paying enough attention to him, your Sheltie will try to get your attention more forcefully. This can also be demonstrated through overall clinginess or neediness.

3. **Chewing or licking himself:** When bored, dogs can start to incessantly chew or lick their own paws or tail to keep themselves occupied. This can cause painful sore spots, and it can even continue until the skin is raw and bleeding. Once this habit is formed, it can be very difficult to break. We're dealing with this problem with Winnie right now—she started licking her paws obsessively, and even though we increased her daily exercise, it had already become a compulsion. Now she won't stop. The main thing we've found that helps is a bitter spray designed for

dogs, which makes her paws taste bad and discourages licking. Offering an alternative toy as a distraction can also be helpful.

NOTE: Paw licking can also be a sign of a food allergy, nutritional deficiency, or an infection or irritation on the skin. You should speak to your vet to rule out other issues before concluding that it's simply a sign of boredom.

4. **Excessive napping or lethargy:** While puppies are generally more prone to destructive behavior when bored than adults, older dogs often nap when they have nothing else to do. Napping is normal, but you shouldn't let your Sheltie sleep all day and become out of shape. One possible sign that your Sheltie is sleeping too much during the day is if he exhibits excessive energy at night when you're trying to go to bed. After all, if he sleeps all day without enough exercise, he isn't going to be tired at bedtime.

5. **Weight gain:** If your Sheltie starts to put on extra pounds—other than the normal weight gain for puppies, of course—it means that your Sheltie's calorie input is exceeding his calorie output by too wide of a margin. If your Sheltie becomes overweight, you will need to discuss his diet and exercise routine with your vet and make any necessary adjustments. We will discuss weight management in depth in a later chapter.

A well-exercised Sheltie, on the other hand, will be happy and content rather than overly needy, will exhibit an age-appropriate level of stamina, will take naps throughout the day while still exhibiting energy at regular intervals, and will channel that energy into the proper activities rather than getting into trouble.

SHELTIES IN BOOKS
Sashi the Sheltie

Linda Greiner adopted her dog, Sashi, from Shetland Sheepdog Placement Services of New Jersey in 2001. Adopting Sashi was such a great experience for Greiner that she was inspired to write a series of children's books, beginning with her debut, *Sashi the Scared Little Sheltie*. This debut novel, published by Brown Books Publishing Group, tells the story of how Sashi was surrendered by her previous owners because of her herding instincts, which caused her to chase everything. The Sashi series now contains several books, including *Sashi Adopts A Brother* and *Sashi and the Puppy Mill Girl*.

CHAPTER EIGHT
Training Your Sheltie

"Obedience training is good for mental stimulation and for teaching tricks. I once had a Sheltie that knew every trick I could think of by the time it was 12 weeks old. They are so smart and pick things up very quickly."

ROSE MARIE DORAN
Granite Gables Shetland Sheepdogs

Photo Courtesy
of Sherry Deeds
BellaRose Shelties

It is helpful to start training your Sheltie as early as possible. Shelties are able to learn at any age, but training can be more difficult once bad habits have been established. After all, Shelties have a mind of their own, and if they're used to being in charge, they may not like being told what to do. However, if you establish a relationship built on trust and respect and integrate proper training based upon that relationship, your Sheltie will be more submissive and eager to please you.

This relational aspect is key in training a Sheltie. Your Sheltie needs to feel secure in your home and be able to trust that you will do what's best for him before he will be willing to submit to your leadership. Building this relationship is twofold. First, you need to establish a loving bond. This is accomplished by spending time with your Sheltie, playing with him, giving him affection, and caring for his needs. This will make your Sheltie feel like part of the family and encourage him to love you in return. Once that love is earned, Shelties love deeply and are fiercely loyal. Second, you need to command respect. This does not mean that you should be domineering or harsh, but your Sheltie needs to understand the dynamics of your relationship—you are the pack alpha, and he needs to submit to you. If you become your Sheltie's friend rather than his master, he will not listen to you or respect you; you'll just become a playmate, like one of his littermates.

Properly training your Sheltie is very important and will benefit both you and your Sheltie. Some of the benefits of proper training include:

1. **Ensuring your Sheltie's safety:** Knowing how to walk on a leash and come when called can help keep your Sheltie safe when you're outside. Proper training can also help prevent your Sheltie from eating harmful substances and will make vet visits go much more smoothly.

2. **Promoting peace within your home:** Establishing clear rules and boundaries within your home will help your homelife be more pleasant for everyone involved, from protecting your floors and furniture, to limiting barking, to simply preventing a daily battle of wills.

3. **Providing mental stimulation:** Training is a form of mental exercise, which will help keep your Sheltie happy and healthy.

4. **Creating a strong bond between you and your Sheltie:** Training provides a wonderful opportunity to bond with your Sheltie and foster a stronger, healthier relationship. While Shelties are fully capable of taking charge, they are generally happiest when they have a firm but loving master. Your Sheltie will want to work for you and please you.

Training your Sheltie will require a lot of time and effort, but it will be worth all the work in the long run.

Setting Clear Expectations

This idea is worth repeating—training your Sheltie will not always be easy. Yes, Shelties are generally intelligent, submissive, and trainable, which will make the process easier than it would be with some breeds; however, this does not mean it will be a straightforward path. While many online articles about "How to Train Your Dog in a Week" can contain some useful tips, these articles can be misleading. Your Sheltie will pick up on some concepts and commands faster than others, but training in general will be a lifelong process. Hopefully, it won't take years to housetrain or teach basic commands like Sit, but you will likely encounter changes throughout your life and your Sheltie's life that will present new situations, such as moving to a

Photo Courtesy of Britt Mertens

new location or having a baby, which will require additional training and adjustment for your Sheltie. Continuing to teach new skills and tricks even as your Sheltie ages will also help keep your dog's mind sharp. Although we will focus on the initial basics for now, it is important to keep in mind that training is not a "quick fix," and you will need to learn and grow with your Sheltie as he matures.

FUN FACT
Badenock Rose

The first Shetland sheepdog to be registered with the English Kennel Club was Badenock Rose in 1909. Rose's registration was announced in the Kennel Gazette in 1909 and was registered as a Shetland Collie. Rose's owner was Mr. W. Wolfenden, and she was born on November 20, 1907.

What to expect from your Sheltie. Shelties are bright and eager to learn, which makes them very trainable, and the more you bond with your Sheltie, the more he will want to work to please you. However, your Sheltie may also become distracted or decide he doesn't want to be told what to do. While Shelties are often very submissive, they also have a stubborn streak and can be very independent at times. They can also be major drama queens.

When Winnie was first learning how to walk on a leash, she would throw temper tantrums. She would lie down on the ground and refuse to move, whining and crying like she was being subjected to the worst torture imaginable.

Raising a Sheltie puppy can at times feel like raising a toddler. It involves a lot of exploring, pressing boundaries, and trying to figure out where you'll draw the line—as well as temper tantrums when that line is drawn too close for their liking. It's the ultimate battle of wills, and unless you want your puppy to end up running your house, which will cause bigger problems down the road, you need to establish firm, clear boundaries and stick to them.

Still, if you put in the time and effort to bond with your Sheltie and provide consistent training, your Sheltie will love you and want to obey you, and he will grow to become a well-mannered adult.

What your Sheltie should expect from you. Training is a two-way street. You can't expect your Sheltie to listen to you if you don't treat your Sheltie well. Again, establishing a strong bond early on is key. Shelties are also extremely sensitive, so if you are too harsh in your words or actions, your Sheltie will respond fearfully or defensively rather than listening to you. Your Sheltie needs to be able to trust that you will be gentle and fair, as well as firm and consistent. This will require a good deal of patience on your part, but as your Sheltie learns to love, trust, and respect you as a master, it will become easier.

Operant Conditioning Basics

"If you teach a Sheltie using love and praise, the sky is the limit. You want your dog to be proud of who he is and what he does. You want him to know that you are his partner. A Sheltie is ruled by his heart."

WANDA FLETCHER
Serenity Shelties

In an article for *Simply Psychology,* Saul McLeod defines operant conditioning as "a method of learning that occurs through rewards and punishments for behavior. Through operant conditioning, an individual

Photo Courtesy
of Rebecca Loyd

makes an association between a particular behavior and a consequence." [1] This term was originally coined by psychologist B. F. Skinner in his research on human behavior, but the concept can also be applied to other creatures, including dogs.

Operant conditioning can be broken down into four main parts: positive reinforcement, negative reinforcement, positive punishment, and negative punishment.

We often assume that *positive* means good and *negative* means bad, but in this case, this categorization is a misconception. In terms of operant conditioning, *positive* means something is added, and *negative* means something is taken away. In a similar manner, *reinforcement* means that a specific behavior is being reinforced or encouraged, while *punishment* means that a behavior is being discouraged. Therefore, the four components of operant conditioning can be defined as follows:

- **Positive reinforcement:** The addition of something, leading to the behavior being repeated more often.

  EXAMPLES:
  - You tell your Sheltie to sit, your Sheltie sits, so you praise your Sheltie and give him a treat. As a result, your Sheltie sits on command more often.
  - Your Sheltie brings back the tennis ball and drops it, so you continue to throw the tennis ball. As a result, your Sheltie brings back the tennis ball and drops it more often.
  - This can also be true of undesired behaviors. For example, your puppy nips you while playing, and you continue to play with him. As a result of this positive reinforcement, your puppy nips while playing more often.

- **Negative reinforcement:** Taking something away, leading to the behavior being repeated more often.

  EXAMPLES:
  - You tell your Sheltie to sit but he doesn't listen, so you apply pressure to his bottom. When your Sheltie sits, you remove the pressure. As a result, your Sheltie sits on command more often.
  - Your Sheltie is pulling on the leash, so you tighten the leash, forcing him to walk next to you. When your Sheltie starts to walk next to you without pulling, you loosen your grip on the leash, removing the added pressure. As a result, your Sheltie starts to walk next to you without pulling more often.

---

1   https://www.simplypsychology.org/operant-conditioning.html

"Shelties absolutely do not do well with physical reprimanding, but will respond to even a slight voice change if correction is needed. A loving pat or treat will be a sufficient reward for correct action."

VIOLET EARL
Earl's Dogpatch

- **Positive punishment:** The addition of something, leading to the behavior being repeated less often.

  EXAMPLES:

  - Your Sheltie won't stop barking at the neighbor, so you tap his nose. As a result, your Sheltie barks at the neighbor less often.
  - Your puppy nips you while playing, so you cry out, "Ow!" You might hold your finger, showing the puppy that you're hurt, so your puppy understands that biting is not acceptable play behavior. As a result, your puppy nips less often while playing.

- **Negative punishment:** Taking something away, leading to the behavior being repeated less often.

  EXAMPLES

  - Your Sheltie barks and jumps on you, trying to get your attention, so you turn away and ignore him, removing your attention, until he calms down. As a result, your Sheltie barks and jumps on you less often.
  - You're trying to teach your Sheltie to sit, but he keeps getting distracted and trying to play with a toy instead. You take the toy away and refuse to play. As a result, he gets distracted during training less often. (Conversely, if you give in and play, it becomes positive reinforcement and teaches your Sheltie to get distracted and try to play during training.)
  - This can also reduce desired behaviors. For example, if your Sheltie figures out that if he comes when you call, it means he has to go inside and stop playing in the yard, he might start to come when called less often.

Often the best approach when training your Sheltie is to use a combination of each of these techniques. Some people try to rely solely on praise, rewarding their puppy when he obeys but avoiding any sort of punishment when he disobeys. However, this approach usually turns out as well as when parents refuse to tell their toddler, "No." It simply results in a spoiled puppy who refuses to listen unless there is a bribe involved. Proper training requires both the encouragement of desired actions and the discouragement of undesired actions.

Dangers of Punishment-Based Training

"Shelties very much want to please their owner, which makes them easier to other breeds that get distracted by their nose or other sights. One thing to be aware of is that Shelties are often noise sensitive so loud noises will usually distract them and sometimes scare them. Try to make interactions positive. Any negative responses to Sheltie behavior should be gentle: Shelties have a long memory."

LAURA WILLSON
Wildwest Shelties

Photo Courtesy
of Robin Berrier

Photo Courtesy
of Allana Kaminski

Still, relying too heavily on punishment—specifically positive punishment— can be even more dangerous than relying solely on praise. Harsh words or actions will easily frighten Shelties, which will make them wary of training sessions for fear of being punished, and their overall anxiety will increase. They might become confused about what they're supposed to do and associate the punishment with the wrong action. In the long run, they'll also likely end up finding loopholes to get around the rules rather than following them. If you are too harsh with your Sheltie, he will likely start to trust you less, which will negatively affect your overall relationship with him, and if this lack of trust worsens, it can make him fear humans in general.

If you do need to punish your Sheltie, remember to be firm but gentle. Shelties are extremely sensitive to tone, so often a firm "No" is all you need. Yelling will only scare your Sheltie. Likewise, you can lightly tap your Sheltie's nose or bottom when he's being blatantly disobedient—though he might give you an offended look—but you should never hit your Sheltie, or else he will become afraid of you or possibly become more defiant. While punishment is occasionally necessary in order to discourage inappropriate actions, Shelties respond best to praise and encouragement. Proper training requires balance, but Shelties typically require a large amount of praise and only some moderate punishment to balance the scales.

Professional Trainers and Obedience Classes

Whether you are a seasoned dog owner or you just adopted your first puppy, the thought of training your Sheltie can be overwhelming, but recruiting the help of a professional can make the process easier. After all, professional trainers are experts in canine psychology and training techniques, so they will be able to guide you through the steps of training your puppy, helping you communicate better with your Sheltie and making sure you stay on track with any major milestones. To find a trainer, you can start by searching online for dog trainers in your area, or you can ask your vet or an experienced friend for their recommendations. Often large pet stores will offer obedience classes, and you can usually find independent trainers and schools in your area as well. When hiring a professional dog trainer, there are two main options: private training or group classes.

Private training offers a more individualized approach since the trainer is able to focus all his attention on you and your puppy. This means the instruction can be tailored to your unique needs, such as addressing a specific behavior problem or helping to smooth over the relationship between your new Sheltie and your other pets. Many trainers also offer flexible scheduling and can even come to your home. However, private training is usually more expensive than group classes, and it doesn't provide the benefit of social-ization, which means your puppy might have more trouble listening to you when there are distractions around. Still, the focused instruction might help your puppy learn more quickly; you will simply need to make an extra effort to socialize your puppy more on your own.

One of the major advantages of group classes is socialization. Going to a group class will expose your Sheltie to a new environment with new smells, people, and dogs. As we discussed earlier, proper socialization is extremely important in order for your puppy to grow into a well-adjusted adult, and group classes offer a wonderful opportunity to start acclimating your puppy to being around other people and dogs. Group classes also teach your puppy to obey when surrounded by distractions, which is a helpful skill to learn. In group classes, the instruction won't be completely tailored to your needs, but you will still be able to ask the trainer any questions you might have. You can also listen to the questions other people ask—questions you may not have thought about otherwise—and benefit from those answers as well. You will just need to make sure your puppy is up-to-date on any necessary vaccinations before attending class.

Whether you choose to hire a private trainer or attend group obedi-ence classes, you need to make sure the instructor's mindset and training approach coincide with your own. You don't want to hire a trainer who rec-ommends training techniques you are not comfortable with. It can also be helpful if the trainer is familiar with Shelties since this breed has so many unique quirks. As always, you should carefully do your research before mak-ing a final decision. You can call and ask questions, and you can see if the trainer offers a free trial class. You can also pay for one class to see if you like the style of instruction before investing in a whole month or more.

Basic Training Timeline

There is no set schedule for training a puppy, but there are a few import-ant milestones you should be aware of. The following timeline is based on the AKC's recommendations[2]:

---

2 Based on an article by Mary Kearl, www.akc.org/expert-advice/training/puppy-training-timeline-teaching-good-behavior-before-its-too-late.

Age	Primary Goals
8-16 weeks	• **Bonding**: Build a loving and trusting relationship with your puppy. • **Socialization**: Your puppy should become comfortable in his home environment, then begin exposure to new people, places, and animals. • **Impulse control**: Start by teaching Sit. Making your puppy sit before meals is a good habit to form—professional trainer Kate Naito likens this to a child learning to say "Please." Your puppy should also eventually learn not to bark or whine for attention.
6 months	• **Housetraining**: This process should start immediately when you bring your puppy home and will take several months to master, but your puppy should have a good handle on it by this age. • **Polite play**: Your puppy should learn how to drop a toy and refrain from biting by this point. • **Crate training**: Your puppy should be comfortable being left alone in a safe, enclosed area for short periods of time. • **Come**: Your puppy should learn to come when called, even if the response time isn't immediate yet.
1 year	• By this point, your Sheltie should have mastered the basic commands of Sit, Lie Down, and Stay. • Your Sheltie should respond to Drop It or Leave It. • Your Sheltie should come when called more quickly and consistently. • Your Sheltie should be able to walk on a leash without pulling

Mastering these basics will help make your home happier and more peaceful, for both you and your Sheltie. If you miss these milestones, you can still work on teaching or improving these skills at a later time, but it might be more difficult if you wait. While older Shelties can still be trained, puppies are generally more malleable since they have not yet developed bad habits or negative associations, so it's generally best to start training as early as possible. We will take a closer look at specific training techniques in the next chapter.

CHAPTER NINE
Basic Obedience Commands

Now that you're well versed in the theory and mindset behind proper dog training, you're ready to take some concrete steps in training your Shetland Sheepdog. Here are some practical tips to keep in mind as you begin:

1. **Stay consistent.** You will need to decide on the house rules before you bring your puppy home—then stick with them. If you don't want your Sheltie on the furniture or you don't want him jumping up to greet you, you will need to enforce these rules from the beginning...with no exceptions. Whatever you allow now will set the precedent for what your Sheltie will continue to do as he ages.

2. **Be firm but gentle.** Remember, while both punishments and reinforcements are necessary for balanced training, being too harsh with your Sheltie will likely scare him and cause more harm than good.

3. **Exercise before training.** Your puppy will have a tough time concentrating on the lesson if he's full of energy. You will need to get his wiggles out first, then work on training when he's calmer and ready to listen.

4. **Let your Sheltie set the pace.** Trying to teach multiple commands all at once will only confuse your puppy. Wait until your Sheltie has fully learned one concept before moving on to something new.

5. **Reward good behavior generously.** Your Sheltie wants to please you, so your praise will encourage him to repeat the desired behavior. Most dogs are also more than willing to work for treats.

6. **End training sessions on a positive note.** If your training session has been filled with corrections and punishments, your puppy will likely be hesitant to train again the next day. Ending the session with lots of praise, attention, and possibly playtime will help form positive associations with training, so your puppy will be happy to continue this training in the future.

If you follow these basic principles, both you and your Sheltie should have a positive experience with training. Now, let's take a look at some specific training techniques.

Photo Courtesy of Livia Sakai

Marker Training

Marker training is a training method that involves associating a specific sound with a desired action. This method was originally developed by B. F. Skinner, the same behaviorist who coined the term "operant conditioning." Most people are familiar with Pavlov ringing a bell before feeding dogs, but although marker training uses some of the same principles, Skinner took this concept a step further. While Pavlov's work dealt with unconscious behavior, such as dogs salivating when they hear a bell, Skinner's work dealt with conscious behavior. Therefore, to place it in terms of operant conditioning, marker training offers positive reinforcement by introducing a specific sound to encourage the continuation of a desired behavior. Today, marker training is one of the most popular methods of dog training because it has been proven to be both effective and humane.

To apply this method, you have two main options: clicker training or verbal markers.

Karen Pryor, an author specializing in behavioral psychology and marine biology, introduced clicker training as a way to apply Skinner's concept of operant conditioning. Clicker training uses a device that makes a noise when you push a button. The idea is to form positive associations with this clicking sound, so hearing this noise will encourage your dog to continue performing a specific action.

To start with, the clicking noise won't mean anything to your Sheltie; you have to condition him to associate the sound with a reward, such as a treat. If you tell your Sheltie to sit and he sits, immediately press the clicker and give a treat. Remember that dogs live in the moment, so unless the reward is immediate, your Sheltie will not understand the connection between the action and the reward. After a while, your Sheltie will be willing to work to earn the click simply because he associates that sound with a coming reward. This means that you can save the treat and praise until the end of the training session rather than giving him a treat every time he obeys.

Once your Sheltie understands the meaning of the clicker, you can also use it to stop unwanted behavior. For example, if your Sheltie refrains from jumping on your guest, press the clicker, so he understands he did something good. If your Sheltie has been having a problem barking excessively, you can create a command, such as Quiet or Shhh, and click when he stops barking.

Since there will likely be times when you want your Sheltie to continue a specific action rather than stopping immediately after the click, such as when you tell him to "Stay" or "Heel," you will need to differentiate between continuation markers and markers indicating completion. For example, you can teach your puppy that if you click once, he needs to remain seated, but if

SHELTIES ON SOCIAL MEDIA
Shelties of Instagram

Shelties of Instagram (@sheltiesofinstagram) is a dedicated Instagram account for featuring Shelties from around the web. Instagram users can tag their Sheltie photos with #smileshelties to potentially have their photos featured on the page. The account is "here to bring your feed smiles, laughter, and awws."

you click twice, he is free to get up. In this case, the double click would act as a release as well as a reward. Just remember that whatever markers you choose need to remain consistent.

VERBAL MARKERS

Verbal markers use the same strategy as clicker training, but they can be more convenient since you don't have to carry a clicker with you everywhere. To use this method, you simply use words as markers instead of clicks, and everything else is the same. You still have to teach your puppy to associate the chosen word with a reward, so you will need to pair the verbal marker with a treat until your Sheltie understands the association.

One of the most common mistakes people make when using verbal markers is being inconsistent with the words they use. Remember that your dog does not speak English; he won't understand that Good Job, Good Boy, and Yes all mean the same thing. If your tone is high pitched and happy, he will understand that you're praising him, but for the purpose of marker training, it is crucial that you remain consistent with your wording. You will need to choose four specific words: One indicating that the desired behavior has been completed successfully, another word indicating that the behavior should be continued until released, a release word, and a word indicating that an undesired behavior should be stopped.

For example:

Yes: Desired action has been completed successfully. Thus, the dog is not obligated to continue performing this action.

Nice: Continuation marker. Continue performing action until released. For example, if you told your dog to "Heel" and he obeys, you can say "Nice" to indicate that he's doing well but needs to keep going.

Free: Release word. For example, if the dog has been told to stay, saying "Free" would indicate that he's able to move freely again.

No: Undesirable behavior needs to stop.

It can be helpful to choose words that you only use during these circumstances rather than vague words, such as Good Boy, which you might use more generally. After all, if you're like me, you'll tell your puppy what a good boy he is even if he's just lying on the ground doing nothing!

Photo Courtesy of Moyra Miller

Basic Commands

Although you now understand how to encourage the repetition of desired behaviors, you might still be wondering how to get your puppy to obey the commands in the first place. Let's take a look at a few basic commands.

Sit

As we discussed earlier, *Sit* will likely be one of the first commands you teach your puppy. Sitting can be a useful skill for your puppy to understand because it provides the opportunity for him to ask for things politely rather than whining. It's a good idea to have your puppy sit before giving him food or when you're putting on his leash when it's time to go outside. Having your puppy sit can also help redirect him if he's getting too hyper or barking excessively.

One method of teaching your puppy to sit is known as *luring*. This technique involves holding a treat in front of your puppy and slowly lifting it up; as he reaches up for it, this action will naturally cause him to sit to avoid falling backwards. As soon as his bottom touches the ground, give the marker (whether a word or a click) and a treat. After a few times, you can also introduce the verbal command and/or hand gesture as he begins to sit, then give the reward. After a while, your Sheltie will begin to associate the command with the action, and the reward will encourage him to obey.

When using the luring method, the key is to hold the treat a proper distance away from the puppy and move slowly. If you hold it too far away, he might jump for it, but if you hold it too close, he might try to bite it out of your hand. Likewise, if you move it too fast, he might back up instead of sitting. If you encounter any of these problems, adjust the way you hold the treat as necessary.

Another common method is known as *capturing*. This technique involves holding a treat in front of your puppy and waiting for him to sit on his own. When he sits, give the marker and a treat, and after a few times, introduce the desired command as he starts to sit. However, the main problem with this method is that your puppy may not end up sitting at all, in which case you will need to revert back to the luring method.

Do NOT use physical force to make your puppy sit down. This might scare and confuse him. The goal is to form associations through gentle reinforcement. Eventually, your puppy will make the connection between the command and the action—and between the action and the reward—without the need for physical force.

Lie Down

You can utilize the same techniques to teach your puppy to lie down as you did to teach him to sit. You can use the luring method by holding a treat in front of your puppy and slowly bringing it to the floor. When he lies down, give the marker and a treat. After a few successful tries, you can introduce the verbal command in addition to the motion of moving your hand downwards as your puppy begins to lie down. You can also use the capturing method by waiting for your puppy to lie down on his own, then employing the same technique. For this method, it can be helpful to begin in a small room free of any distractions, such as a bathroom. Still, your puppy might not end up lying down voluntarily at all, so this method may not work.

Once your puppy is used to obeying the respective command in a distraction-free area, practice both the *Sit* and *Lie Down* commands in different environments, such as when you're outside on a walk or at the pet store. This skill will train your puppy to listen to you even when surrounded by distractions.

Again, do NOT physically force your puppy to lie down.

Come

"The most important command of all is 'come'. This command takes time & consistency, but in the event of a crisis or danger, you need them to stop what they are doing & return to you!"

SHERRY DEEDS
BellaRose Shelties

Being able to come when called is an important skill for your Sheltie to learn. Beyond making everyday interactions easier, having a reliable recall might save your Sheltie's life one day if the backyard gate is accidentally left open or he somehow ends up off-leash. However, in order to come to you, your puppy has to give up whatever game or exploration he is currently engaged in, so to train him to come on command, you will need to form as many positive associations with being near you as possible. The fact that you should already be bonding with your puppy will be helpful here.

To practice this skill, start by moving a few feet away from the puppy, hold out a treat, and once the puppy starts to move toward you, say your chosen command. When the puppy reaches you, give the treat and lots of praise. The trick here is to only say the command once you're sure the puppy is already coming toward you. If you give the command when the puppy isn't paying attention, you can fall into the trap of repeating the word so many times without results that it loses its meaning. Your puppy needs to only associate the word with the action.

You should start with short distances in a distraction-free environment, then gradually increase the distance and number of distractions. If you don't have a fenced-in yard, you can use a long leash and leave it loose as your puppy explores, so you can practice the recall safely in different environments. Once your puppy starts to get the hang of it, you can also try playing games such as chase, where you run and have your puppy chase you, using the cue word for Come once he starts to move with you. After a few paces, stop and reward him for following you. (This game can also be a helpful trick if your puppy gets loose—instead of chasing your puppy, which will only encourage him to run away more because he thinks it's fun, try running the other direction and encourage your puppy to chase you.)

Once your puppy starts to have a more reliable recall, you can also play hide-and-seek by going into a different room and calling for your puppy, then rewarding him once he finds you. The goal is to make training fun, and more specifically, to make coming to you fun and worthwhile.

A common issue people face when teaching recall is that their dogs stop responding to the command, even if they previously had a reliable recall, because they form negative associations with coming on command. For example, if your Sheltie is playing in the backyard and every time you call him, he has to come inside and stop playing, he might start ignoring your command because what he's doing is far more interesting than what you want him to do. This association might extend to other circumstances as well, resulting in your Sheltie's constant refusal to come. To prevent this issue, it can be helpful to occasionally practice calling your Sheltie, then reward him for coming and let him continue what he was doing. You could also call your Sheltie to come inside, then play with him inside. Although this won't always be possible, the key is to prevent your Sheltie from developing the mindset of Come meaning all the fun is over.

It is also extremely important to never punish your Sheltie for coming to you. Even if you're frustrated with him for taking a long time to come, still reward him when he finally reaches you. If you scold him, you will only make him more hesitant to come the next time you call. Likewise, if your puppy gets into trouble, do not call him to you before punishing him. Your puppy needs to associate coming to you with safety and fun. If he thinks he will be punished if he comes when you call, he will stop obeying this command altogether.

Stay

The command *Stay* can be a difficult one for puppies to master. After all, you've just taught your Sheltie that being with you is the greatest thing in the world, and everything in his little body wants to follow you when you walk away. However, now you want him to stay in the same position until released.

To accomplish this, have your puppy sit or lie down, tell him to stay, then give your chosen release word almost immediately afterwards. Make sure your release word stays consistent, such as *Free* or *Okay*. If your puppy doesn't respond to it right away, you can clap or talk to your puppy in a high-pitched, excited tone, indicating it's alright for him to move, but do not always call for your puppy to come afterwards or else he will simply anticipate the recall command rather than paying attention to the Stay and release cues. You also should not hold a treat when you tell your puppy to stay because this will naturally encourage him to come to you.

Once your puppy starts to understand the concept of *Stay* and the release word, you can gradually increase the length of time before the release, as well as the distance between you and your puppy. Go slowly—the duration of the stay should only be increased a few seconds at a time, and you should only back up one step at a time. If your puppy moves before he is released, try again and go back to a time and distance he was able to accomplish successfully. The more successful the training is, the more it will stick in your puppy's mind, so you should not push him to progress faster than he is ready.

Eventually, you will be able to practice walking away from your puppy while facing him as well as turning your back on him, and you can start introducing other distractions and practicing the command in different environments. Then, after lots of practice, you will even be able to leave the room without him moving from his position. When you come back and give the release word, give him a treat and lots of praise.

Give/Drop

Teaching your Sheltie to drop something he's holding in his mouth can be very important, especially if he ends up getting ahold of something dangerous or valuable. However, you don't want to wait until an emergency situation to practice this skill. Instead, you should teach this command while playing with a tug toy or ball. This can also be helpful if your puppy has been having difficulty giving the ball back when playing fetch.

To encourage your puppy to drop the toy, trade it for a treat. Hold the treat in front of his nose and wait for him to open his mouth to reach for the treat instead. Once he drops the toy, give him the treat. After he has successfully dropped the toy a few times, you can start to introduce the desired *Drop* command. You can also continue playing with the puppy afterwards, so he understands that he isn't giving up the toy forever.

Most dogs will be willing to give up a toy in exchange for a treat, but if your Sheltie is more motivated by play, you can also try exchanging the toy for a different toy. Make sure that the new toy is more desirable, such as a favorite stuffed animal or tennis ball instead of a less interesting chew toy. Whether you use a treat or toy, repeat this process and practice several times a day until your Sheltie will drop the toy on command without a bribe.

Do not wrestle any object out of your puppy's mouth unless it is an emergency, or else you could hurt his mouth or cause him to choke. It might also turn into a game of tug-of-war. If your puppy has something he shouldn't and is trying to play keep away, you can go into the kitchen and loudly open the bag of treats, which should encourage him to come running and drop whatever he is holding. Only forcibly open your puppy's mouth if he's about to eat something that will seriously harm him and he won't drop it on command.

Walking on a Leash

Walking on a leash without pulling is a skill that requires training and encouragement, just like sitting or coming. It can be difficult for some puppies. After all, their freedom is being restricted, so they might protest this loss of autonomy by refusing to move, even if they would otherwise follow you willingly.

When Winnie was first learning how to walk on a leash, she would throw temper tantrums, crying and falling on the ground dramatically. Even today, she will pout and throw little fits when we put her harness on her because she knows she cannot slip out of the harness like she can with her collar. She values her independence!

While this reaction is normal and understandable, you want to minimize any negative associations with the collar and leash. Even wearing a collar can feel strange at first, so you need to be patient and give your puppy time to adjust.

It can be helpful to start by putting the collar on your Sheltie around mealtime or playtime, so the puppy is distracted and happy. If he starts to fixate on it and scratch at it, you can divert his attention with food or a toy. Once the puppy is used to wearing a collar, you can try attaching a leash, but don't try to hold it just yet. Your puppy might try to chew on it, or he might plop himself down and refuse to budge. Try to distract him and play with him in the house or the backyard, letting the leash drag behind him freely. You want him to grow comfortable with it and associate the leash with fun, rather than viewing it as scary and restricting. However, carefully supervise your puppy whenever he wears a leash to make sure it doesn't get snagged or tangled.

Once your puppy is comfortable with having a collar and leash around his neck, you can try picking up the leash and holding it. Start to walk, encouraging your puppy to follow you, and praise him and give a treat if he does. If he refuses to move, go a few steps away and then stop, kneel, and hold out a treat. When your puppy comes up to you, praise him and give the treat. Repeat this process, practicing walking around your house or yard where your puppy is already comfortable and familiar with the environment.

Once your puppy is comfortable walking with you at home, you can venture out into the neighborhood. Keep a short leash at first; you'll be able to provide more slack once your Sheltie is better trained, but for now, a short leash will help your puppy learn to walk next to you rather than wandering off. Having him walk beside you, rather than in front or behind you, will also help prevent him from getting distracted. Make sure you give plenty of praise and a treat when your puppy exhibits proper behavior.

You should not yank on the leash. Instead, your focus should be on rewarding good behavior. If your puppy doesn't want to leave a certain spot, you can move a few paces away, kneel, and encourage him to follow you by holding out a treat. Praise him when he comes to you, then keep going.

If your puppy tries to pull on the leash, there are two main responses: you can stand still and refuse to move until your puppy comes back to you, or you can turn and walk the opposite direction, forcing your puppy to turn and follow you. If he tries to lunge after something, like a person or squirrel, or starts barking at another dog, you can turn and walk in the opposite direction until the distraction passes. If possible, it can also help to be proactive and hold out a treat when you notice him start to fixate on a specific trigger, then reward him when he turns and focuses his attention on you instead.

A Sheltie's Intuition

"Shelties are very smart & quick learners. Because their willingness to please they are capable of doing a multitude of things. They excel in agility and if they are built right, are great for confirmation. They are great listeners & give great comfort, so they make fantastic therapy dogs."

SHERRY DEEDS
BellaRose Shelties

As we've discussed, training your puppy will take a lot of time and patience; however, you might be surprised by your Sheltie's intuition. Shelties are very intelligent and attuned to their master's emotions, tones, and desires.

We often talk to Winnie, and she'll know exactly what we want, even if she has never been trained to recognize a specific command. Don't be surprised if your Sheltie also learns to recognize words and associations without training. Our command to fetch the tennis ball is *Get It, Get It,* but Winnie also learned the word Ball before long. We started spelling it out when we didn't want her to notice, but now she recognizes that as well!

Shelties' intelligence, intuition, memory, and desire to please their master make them extremely trainable. Your responsibility is to capitalize on this potential by providing the training, which will then provide mental stimulation to make your Sheltie happy and healthy, establish you as the pack alpha, and help you bond with your Sheltie.

CHAPTER TEN
Dealing With Unwanted Behaviors

"Shelties are extremely smart. So teach them tricks or agility, anything to keep their minds busy or else they will figure out their own things to get into."

MARY LOU FOSTER
Loveable Shelties

E ven if you put in the time and effort to train your Sheltie, there are going to be some bumps along the road. Although inconvenient or undesirable for you, many "bad" behaviors your Sheltie may exhibit

are instinctual or derived from an unmet need. Two of the most common behavior problems in Shetland Sheepdogs as a breed are excess barking, which comes from a protective instinct as watchdogs, and separation anxiety due to the strong attachment they form with their master.

The definition of "bad" behavior also varies widely depending on the household or individual. In our home, Winnie is allowed to sleep on our bed or the couch, but in a different house, a dog getting on the furniture might be considered a bad habit that needs to be corrected.

Before bringing home your puppy, you need to make sure everyone in your house is on the same page regarding the household rules. If your spouse allows the puppy on the bed when you're not around, but you don't want the puppy to get on the bed, this habit will be much harder to break. The rules need to be enforced consistently to prevent any confusion for the puppy.

Preventing Problem Behaviors

"Be consistent. If you wouldn't tolerate a behavior in an adult, don't give into puppy cuteness and let them get away with it when you first get your puppy. It's not fair to the puppy when suddenly you decide that the little darling chewing on your fingers is not a good thing."

LAURA WILLSON
Wildwest Shelties

Whenever possible, proactively preventing unwanted behaviors is much easier than trying to stop them after they have become habits. This can be accomplished in part by enforcing the rules consistently from day one. For example, if you start feeding your dog table scraps, then stop because you notice he's becoming overweight, the begging will continue even though the rules have changed.

Another major factor in preventing problem behaviors is making sure your Sheltie receives adequate exercise. Many common behavior problems occur simply because the puppy is bored. If your puppy does not have an appropriate outlet for all his excess energy, he will find ways to entertain himself, which might include chewing your nice leather belt or digging up your garden. It is your responsibility to make sure your Sheltie receives enough exercise through playtime, walks, and job-oriented tasks. Refer back to Chapter Seven to ensure that your Sheltie is receiving enough of each type of mental and physical exercise.

Fixing Bad Habits

But what do you do when despite your best efforts, your puppy picks up an undesirable habit? Some habits are harder to break than others, but it's not necessarily too late. Let's take a look at some of the most common behavior issues in dogs.

FUN FACT
The President's Dogs

Calvin Coolidge, the 30th president of the United States, had many dogs during his life, including a Sheltie. Coolidge once said, "Any man who does not like dogs and want them about does not deserve to be in the White House." After the death of the president's collie, Prudence Prim, a pair of children from Michigan sent the presidential family a new dog named Diana. Diana was a Shetland sheepdog. She was quickly renamed Calamity Jane, after the American frontierswoman, by the first lady. Calamity Jane was notorious for getting dirty. The president even had a permanent dog bathtub installed in the White House for the Sheltie, who needed to be bathed nearly every day.

Chewing

Chewing is a natural instinct for dogs, and it even promotes good dental health. However, it can become a problem when your Sheltie decides to use your shoes, furniture, or throw pillows as chew toys. The first step in stopping this problem is understanding why your Sheltie is chewing items in the first place. Puppies often feel the strong urge to chew due to teething or even due to curiosity and exploration, like babies who put everything within reach into their mouths. If an older dog suddenly starts chewing various objects, it's often a sign of an underlying issue, such as boredom or separation anxiety, which you will need to address.

The best ways to prevent unwanted chewing are to provide adequate exercise and offer an alternative chew toy. As we've discussed, your Sheltie might start chewing random objects if he's bored or has too much energy. He needs to receive ample exercise to keep him from finding undesirable ways to entertain himself. Likewise, you will not be able to completely curb your puppy's chewing instinct, so you need to provide an appropriate outlet for this impulse. Keep in mind that it might take a few tries before you find a chew toy your puppy likes—Shelties can be picky—so feel free to experiment with a few different types and don't get discouraged if he rejects the first ones you buy.

If you catch your puppy chewing on something he shouldn't, interrupt him and reprimand him with a firm "No," so he understands he's not supposed to do this. Take the object away and give him a chew toy instead. Praise him if he starts chewing on the new toy. After a while, he should learn what he is and isn't allowed to chew on.

If the inappropriate chewing persists and it's not possible to move the target object out of the puppy's reach, you can also consider using a nontoxic deterrent spray designed for pets. These sprays use all natural ingredients that won't hurt your puppy or your furniture, such as apple cider vinegar or lemon juice, but they make the object taste bad, thereby discouraging your puppy from putting it in his mouth.

Digging

While some dogs were bred to dig and hunt down small animals, Shelties are not natural diggers. However, this does not mean your Sheltie will automatically be immune to this habit. If your Sheltie starts digging in your backyard or garden, it likely means that he is bored and needs more exercise or a job to entertain his mind. He might have also observed you gardening, so he's now trying to copy your behavior. The best way to prevent digging is to give your Sheltie a different task to occupy his mind and energy. If you provide adequate mental and physical energy, your Sheltie likely will not feel the urge to continue digging.

Shelties are typically not prone to digging under fences, but if your dog happens to be the exception and you notice him start to dig holes near the base of the fence, you can bury chicken wire along the fence line or place large, partially buried rocks by the bottom of the fence. It's better to be safe than find out your pup has escaped.

Separation Anxiety

Separation anxiety is one of the most common issues Sheltie owners face. After all, you've spent all this time building a strong bond with your pup, and now he doesn't want to be away from you. Shelties tend to be fiercely loyal and loving toward their master, which can lead to intense anxiety when that person leaves. Shelties are also naturally sensitive and prone to being nervous, which can exacerbate the issue.

Signs of separation anxiety include nervousness while you get ready to leave, such as following you from room to room while whining and shaking, incessant barking that begins as soon as you leave, pawing at the door, and chewing furniture or other household objects while you're away. Your Sheltie might pace nervously or engage in self-destructive behavior, such as biting at his paws. Even if he's housetrained, he might also regress to having accidents in the house when you're gone. Upon your return, your Sheltie will likely become excessively excited, barking and jumping around, and acting like you've been gone for years.

Here are some ways to help mitigate separation anxiety in your Sheltie:

1. **Keep your departures and arrivals as low-key as possible.** If you have long, drawn-out goodbyes and get super hyped up and excited upon your arrival home, you're simply confirming the idea that leaving and coming back is a BIG deal. It can be tempting to go along with your dog's excitement, especially when he seems so happy to see you, but if you remain calm and laid back instead, it will help him remain calm in the long run. As a general rule, you should never act overly sympathetic when your Sheltie gets anxious or upset because it will reinforce the idea that he has something to be upset about. Remaining cool and confident is often the best way to reassure him that everything is alright.

2. **Switch up your routine before leaving.** If you follow the same routine every morning before you leave for work, your Sheltie will pick up on that routine, and it might trigger anxiety because he knows you're going to be gone the rest of the day. Try changing what you do and the order in which you do things before you leave in order to avoid setting off this alert.

3. **Practice leaving without actually leaving.** If you notice that the jingling of your keys when you pick them up triggers your Sheltie's anxiety, try picking them up occasionally and setting them back down without going anywhere. This will help acclimate him to the sound and teach him that it's not a big deal. You can also try going out the door, waiting a few seconds, then coming right back inside, so your Sheltie learns that you leaving the house doesn't mean you'll be gone forever.

Photo Courtesy
of Esther Wijma

4. **Practice having alone time.** If your Sheltie panics whenever he is left alone, try practicing being in a different room, out of his sight, a few times a day. You can start small, only five to ten seconds at a time, then slowly build up to a half-hour over a few weeks. This will help him adjust to the idea of being by himself, without you ever leaving the house.

5. **Exercise before you leave.** Your Sheltie will have a much harder time remaining calm if he's a bundle of energy. Going for a walk or playing fetch before you leave will help burn off excess energy and leave him feeling tired, content, and relaxed. He might even sleep most of the time you're gone!

6. **Provide opportunities for independent play.** You want your Sheltie to remain distracted and occupied while you're gone. As we've established, boredom tends to lead to mischief. Leave out chew toys or other toys designed to be used independently, such as a KONG ball filled with peanut butter.

7. **Provide background noise.** Leaving on classical music or a talk show can be comforting because the noise makes your Sheltie feel less alone.

8. **Don't be gone too long.** Even if you arrange for someone to take care of your Sheltie while you're gone, don't forget that he wants to spend time with YOU. You're the person he's bonded with, so you're the person he wants to spend time with and craves attention from. Even if his physical needs are met, if you're never around, he will become overly anxious when you leave and fervently cling to you when you're home.

Your Sheltie will also likely bond most strongly with one specific person in your household. Winnie is most strongly bonded with my husband, and she sometimes exhibits signs of separation anxiety when he leaves even if I'm still in the house with her. Being alone isn't the only trigger for separation anxiety in Shelties; it's being away from their favorite person.

Nipping and Mouthing

Puppies are naturally mouthy and might nip during play, so they need to be taught proper bite inhibition. When they're with their littermates, the other puppies will yelp and refuse to continue playing if one of them bites down too hard. You can employ this same technique if your puppy tries to nip during play.

You will need to decide what the boundaries will be—some people are okay with light contact as long as the puppy doesn't bite down, while others prefer no tooth contact at all. If your puppy crosses this boundary, cry out and hold your hand, indicating that you're hurt. This should startle your puppy into stopping what he's doing. Due to Shelties' sensitive nature, your puppy will likely become concerned, and he might even try to lick your hand to make it feel better. If he stops or licks you, praise him, then continue playing.

If the play biting persists, you can try employing the "time-out" technique. If your puppy nips you, cry out in pain, then turn around and completely ignore your puppy for ten to twenty seconds. Do not look at him, speak to him, or touch him. If this doesn't work, you can also try leaving the room for a little while. He should get the message before long.

The same principle applies if you find that your Sheltie tries to nip at your heels to "herd" you. You can cry out to let your puppy know he hurt you, but then turn into a statue and don't move or engage with him. If you continue walking when your Sheltie is nipping at your heels, you will encourage the behavior. By refusing to move, you will let him know that he can't nip you to tell you where to go.

Do not use physical force to punish nipping. This often encourages further aggression and ends up exacerbating the problem. Taking away what he wants most—your attention and play—is far more effective. Also, make sure you provide toys that he is allowed to gnaw on instead of your fingers and toes, so he has an appropriate outlet for that chewing instinct.

Older dogs shouldn't have as much of an issue with nipping. Shelties are not generally mouthy beyond puppyhood, and they are very rarely aggressive. However, if there's a slip-up and your Sheltie accidentally nips you during play, follow the same steps listed above. Your Sheltie will likely grow concerned and want to take care of you.

Jumping on People

While many people don't mind having a small puppy jumping up to greet them, jumping is often considered bad manners for a dog and, depending on the size of your Sheltie, can become more of an issue as he grows. Still, consistency is important, and if you don't want your Sheltie to jump on people as an adult, you will need to enforce this rule from the beginning.

Dogs jump up to greet people because they want attention and can't contain their excitement. Therefore, if you want to discourage this behavior, you will need to take away the thing your Sheltie wants most: your attention. Negative attention is still attention, so even if you push him down when he jumps on you, you're actually still encouraging the action. Instead, if your Sheltie jumps on you, turn your back to him, cross your arms, and don't look at him or interact with him. Continue to ignore him until he stops jumping, then reward him for keeping all his paws on the ground by petting him and greeting him more enthusiastically.

If your Sheltie continues to have trouble with this, it can also be helpful to insert a different command, such as *Sit*, since it is impossible for your Sheltie to sit down and jump on you at the same time. When your Sheltie jumps, tell him to "Sit," then pet him and give a treat if he obeys. Having your Sheltie sit when greeting people can also be a good habit to form for when you have visitors or meet people on the street, since some people might not be keen to have a dog jump on them and might not be willing to play along with the ignoring tactic.

Jumping on Furniture

Depending on the rules of your house, you might not want your Sheltie to get on your couch, bed, or other furniture. In this case, it will be necessary to teach him the *Off* command. After all, having him jump down himself is much nicer than forcing him down. Shelties can be stubborn, though, so don't be surprised if your pup tests the limits even after he understands the rules.

Winnie is allowed on all our couches except for one special chair, and she is very aware of this fact. The fact that it's forbidden makes her want to sit there even more. I sometimes come home to find her on it, so I know she sits there when she's home alone. One time, she even jumped up when we were in the room, and when we told her to get down, she stood with her back turned to us, pretending not to hear the command.

Shelties are persistent, so you will have to be even more persistent. And once again, consistency is key. If you let your Sheltie get away with it once, or if someone else in your house allows him on the furniture, the habit will be much harder to break.

When your Sheltie jumps up on the furniture, firmly give the *Off* command and lure him down with a treat. As soon as all four paws are back on the ground, praise him and give the treat. After a while, he should start to respond to the command without needing the lure, and you can start to fade out the treats by giving verbal praise instead and only giving treats intermittently.

A problem might arise, however, if your Sheltie figures out that if he jumps on the furniture then jumps down, he gets a reward. This might cause him to start jumping on the furniture even more. In this case, it can be helpful to give a different command, such as *Sit* or *Lie Down*, after he jumps down and before giving the treat, so your Sheltie does not make the connection between jumping on the furniture and getting a treat.

Also, keep in mind that Shelties love comfort, so by jumping on your couch or bed, your pup might simply be looking for a soft place to sleep. If you don't want to allow him on your furniture, you need to give him an alternative option. Invest in a comfy dog bed and some soft blankets, and your Sheltie will be happy without having to steal your seat.

Inappropriate Behavior with Other Pets

If you have multiple animals in your home, your pets may start to experience sibling rivalry. If you have a cat, the best solution is simply to give the cat a means of escape by providing high-up places where the dog can't reach, and keep the cat's food out of reach as well.

If you have multiple dogs, the rivalry can be more complicated. Dogs are pack animals, and they will naturally fall into a hierarchy. One of the dogs will inevitably become alpha—you don't have a say in which one—and your job is to be alpha over all of them. Still, fights may break out from time to time. Sometimes the problem occurs because people bring a new puppy into the home without the proper preparations, hoping the pack dynamic will eventually settle on its own. To avoid this mistake, refer to Chapter Four to review the proper way to introduce a new puppy to your current dog.

Also, keep in mind that dogs often roughhouse during play, and other times the scuffles are simply their way of figuring out the dominance hierarchy. You do not need to intervene every time unless one of the dogs is excessively bullying the other one or there is a genuine concern that one of them will get hurt.

If a fight does break out, stay calm. Panicking or yelling will only amplify the dogs' negative response since they will feed off your energy. Also, remember to NEVER grab the head or collar of a fighting dog or insert your hands into the middle of the fight—this will put you at substantial risk of getting bitten. Instead, try to distract them and break their focus. Sometimes a loud noise like a car horn will startle them into stopping what they're doing, or throwing a heavy blanket on top of them might cause them to stop long enough for you to separate them. If nothing else works and you have two adults present, you can also try the wheelbarrow technique, but keep in mind that this method is potentially dangerous, depending on the severity of the fight. For this method, each adult should slowly approach one of the dogs from behind and carefully grab hold of its hind legs. Simultaneously, walk backwards in a circular path, forcing the dogs to walk on their front paws to maintain their balance. Lead them into separate rooms, then close the doors.

However, keeping the dogs isolated from each other is not a practical long-term strategy. After all, they live in the same house and will end up together eventually, and proper socialization is important for both dogs' overall well-being. In extreme cases, when the dogs cannot stand the sight of each other, you can try conditioning them to be happy being together.

To accomplish this, you will need another adult to help, so one person can be with each dog. Hold each dog on a leash at a distance where they will not lunge at each other, but they can still see each other; then, when the other dog is within sight, start feeding your dog a high-value treat or food item. The other person should do the same with the other dog.

After a little while, move the dogs out of each other's sight and stop feeding them. Repeat these steps, and after a while, the sight of the other dog will make the dog you're holding look at you excitedly and anticipate a treat. Then, you can start slowly bringing the dogs closer together and adding other stimuli, such as movement or commands like Sit. Let the dogs set the pace and back up when necessary, but eventually they should become more comfortable being around each other and even become happy at the sight of the other dog. Once this is achieved, you can start taking the dogs on walks together while maintaining an appropriate distance between them to prevent them from becoming triggered. The goal is to acclimate them to the idea of being together.

Removing other potential triggers at home, such as fights over food, can also be achieved through strategies such as feeding them in separate rooms or locking them in their separate crates during mealtimes.

Don't forget to also spend equal time with each dog. Your attention is a valued resource, and if you start ignoring your current dog in favor of the new puppy, it might trigger fights as well.

If you find that one of your dogs continues to display aggression, don't hesitate to recruit the help of a professional. An aggressive dog is a big problem, and you can easily find yourself in over your head. A private dog trainer will be able to come to your home to help you sort out the balance between your pets safely and effectively.

Barking

"Shelties by nature love to hear themselves bark. So, we teach the commands 'bark' and 'no bark'. When they are bored they will run the fence & bark. This may drove neighbors crazy, so don't leave them unattended outside for long periods of time."

SHERRY DEEDS
BellaRose Shelties

Since Shelties are alert watchdogs, barking is one of the most common behavior issues they exhibit. They usually do not bark for no reason, but they will alert you to anyone or anything they perceive as a potential threat—including your neighbors, any nearby dogs, the mailman, any unidentified noises, and sometimes even a suspicious-looking shadow. While your Sheltie might feel proud of himself for protecting his home so valiantly, this barking will likely become a problem for you and your neighbors.

I'll be honest here...I don't have a perfect cure-all solution for you. Barking is an instinct that is deeply engrained within Shelties. There's a good chance that you'll never be able to stop it completely, but hopefully, you'll be able to reduce it enough to preserve the peace within your home and neighborhood.

There are two main methods for ending a barking frenzy within your home. The first involves teaching distinct commands for *Speak* and *Quiet.*

Photo Courtesy of Catrina Mehltretter

Teaching your Sheltie to speak should be relatively easily. Simply do something you know will trigger barking, such as knocking on the table or getting hyped up and excited, then praise him and give a treat when he barks. He will quickly learn that barking gets rewarded. After a couple times, introduce the Speak command when he barks, then give the reward. Start refusing to give the treat unless the barking is accompanied by the *Speak* command, so your Sheltie learns that only barking on command gets rewarded, not any barking. Once your Sheltie understands how to bark on cue, you can introduce your chosen *Quiet* command, such as *Hush* or *Shhh,* by telling him to bark then holding out a treat for him to sniff. When he stops barking to sniff the treat quietly, give the Quiet cue and then give the treat. Repeat this process, slowly increasing the amount of time in between giving the *Quiet* cue and giving the treat.

For the next few days, use the *Speak and Quiet* commands any time your Sheltie barks to reinforce their meaning. Once he gets the hang of it, you'll be able to use the *Quiet* cue to end any barking outbursts, and Speak can simply remain a fun trick to practice occasionally.

The second method utilizes positive punishment to discourage barking. Remember, in terms of operant conditioning, positive punishment involves the addition of something, which leads to the behavior being repeated less often. The idea here is to introduce a loud, annoying noise whenever your Sheltie starts barking. Some people rattle coins in a can, but you could also use a bell or horn or anything else that makes a loud noise. However, do not yell, or your Sheltie will think you're joining in the barking and bark even more. You need to remain calm and collected in order for this to work. Whenever your Sheltie barks, make the loud noise. This should startle him into being quiet. When he stops barking and looks in the direction of the noise (in other words, at you), you can then introduce positive reinforcement by giving a treat. This will teach your Sheltie that barking leads to a loud, icky noise, but being quiet and looking at you leads to a reward.

Some people use bark collars to discourage barking, which also applies the principle of positive punishment. Some of these collars vibrate when the dog barks, while others emit a high-pitched noise that can only be heard by dogs, not humans. (There are also shock collars, but these are inhumane. After all, if the dog barks, he gets shocked. Then, if he yelps because he's in pain, he gets shocked again. This can make an already timid Sheltie even more fearful.) The point of bark collars is to teach the dog that if he barks, he gets an unpleasant response. They're not always effective, however, and even if they work, the dog might learn that he can get away with barking whenever he's not wearing the collar. We tried using a vibrating bark collar with Winnie, and it did nothing; still, other people have had success with this method.

When to Call a Professional

Dealing with behavior problems in your Sheltie can be difficult and overwhelming. If you try all the methods listed above with no success, you might want to consider turning to a professional for help. A professional dog trainer will be able to help you pinpoint the root cause of the issue and walk you through various methods of solving it.

Of course, you don't have to wait to hire a trainer as a last resort. Hiring a trainer as soon as you start having problems can be helpful since the trainer can help you nip the issue in the bud. After all, the longer the problem persists, the more firmly established the bad habits will become, and the harder these habits will be to break. A professional trainer will be able to help bridge the communication gap between you and your Sheltie more quickly and easily, which will help save a lot of time and frustration.

CHAPTER ELEVEN
Nutrition

Most dog owners want the absolute best for their fur babies, including the best available food. Providing proper nutrition is crucial in order to maintain your Sheltie's overall health, including muscle tone, skin and coat health, proper digestion, and strength of immunity. Dogs need to ingest a proper balance of all the basic nutrients—water, protein, fats, carbohydrates, vitamins, and minerals—in order to live long, happy, healthy lives.

Photo Courtesy of Kelsey Gordon

Choosing a Quality Commercial Food

"Feed a well-balanced diet. Raw foods and Grain-free foods are really not good for Shelties. Through the years I have always loved and trusted Purina products the best. Do not buy super cheap miscellaneous brand dog foods. Stick with reliable brands."

SUZI BEACHAM
Shalamar Shelties

Walking into the food aisle at a pet store can be an overwhelming experience for first-time dog owners. All the brands claim to provide the necessary nutrients for your pup, but which one is the best? Can you simply pick the most budget-friendly option and call it a day?

There are many areas where you can cut back on costs when purchasing pet supplies, but diet is not one of them. The cheapest dog food brands are cheap for a reason—they often skimp on ingredients, using low quality products from sketchy sources and including extra grain as fillers instead of meat. If you give your Sheltie this food, he is going to be malnourished and will likely have health problems as a result.

When choosing your Sheltie's food, you should look for protein-based brands that use natural, clearly labelled ingredients. You should always avoid food that includes any of the following ingredients:

1. **"Meat by-products."** When the meat ingredients are labelled as "by-products," they typically include all the parts of an animal that are deemed unsuitable for human consumption—in other words, all the leftovers from the slaughterhouses, such as feet, heads, beaks, bones, feathers, and even diseased meat and garbage.

2. **Generic "Meat" Meal.** The exact type of meat should be listed, such as chicken or beef. If the ingredient is listed as "meat" or "bone" meal, this can sometimes include roadkill or euthanized pets.

3. **Artificial preservatives, sweeteners, or coloring.** Examples include but are not limited to BHA, BHT, propylene glycol, and grain fragments.

Instead, you should look for food that has a whole meat listed as the top ingredient, along with other meats or specifically labelled meat meals ("meal" means it is a condensed form of the meat with most of the moisture removed), fruits, vegetables, and whole grains, not refined grain products. Natural preservatives, such as tocopherols (Vitamin E) and Vitamin C, are also good ingredients.

Wet vs Dry Food. Pet owners often debate whether wet or dry food is better for their dogs, but each option has advantages and disadvantages. The advantages of dry food are clear: it is more convenient and cost efficient. You can typically buy dry food in larger quantities, and it does not expire as quickly. Some dry foods are also designed to promote dental health by scraping plaque and tartar buildup from teeth while the dog chews. However, depending on the brand, dry food can contain more carbohydrates and artificial additives than wet food.

Wet food typically contains more protein and healthy fat than dry food, which makes it more nutritious. Wet food also keeps dogs more hydrated, which can be helpful if you live in a hot climate or if your dog doesn't drink much, but fresh water should still be constantly available. Wet food can be an especially good option for picky eaters, dogs with dietary problems, or older dogs who have trouble chewing. However, since it has to be refrigerated, it is less convenient than dry food, and it is usually more expensive.

You can also try mixing wet and dry food to reap the benefits of both, but since different brands of food are formulated differently, you will need to stay consistent with which brand you use. Speak to your vet to see which type of food would be best for your Sheltie and make sure he is receiving all the nutrients he needs.

Shelties are often prone to having sensitive stomachs, so you will have to be especially careful what you feed your pup. You might have to try several types of food before you find one that doesn't upset your Sheltie's stomach or invest in a food designed for sensitive bellies. Signs your Sheltie is not digesting his food properly include throwing up and having difficult or irregular bowel movements.

Homemade Diets

"If you feed a high-quality food, you should not need to give your dog any supplements. Keep an eye on coat quality. Is it shiny and does it feel nice? That's a good hint that the food you are feeding is suitable for your Sheltie."

LAURA WILLSON
Wildwest Shelties

Some people prefer to avoid the processed food from a pet store altogether and instead feed their dog whole foods they prepare themselves. This approach can sometimes be more cost efficient, and some people believe that whole foods are healthier for the dog. However, this task should not be taken on lightly. Cooking for your dog is a very time-consuming process. Also, while good commercial dog foods are specially formulated to contain all the nutrients necessary for a healthy diet, homemade diets can be more difficult to navigate successfully. If you plan to feed your Sheltie a homemade diet, you will need to do extensive research on the various nutrients your dog needs, and you will need to consult with a canine nutrition expert to ensure your pup is receiving a healthy and well-balanced diet.

Raw diets have recently risen in popularity since they mimic a dog's natural biological diet of raw meat, bones, and vegetable scraps, and they exclude all grains. Advocates claim the raw diet gives dogs more energy, healthier coats and skin, and cleaner teeth. However, many experts caution against feeding household dogs raw meat because it contains harmful bacteria, which can make them sick. Owners who feed their dog raw meat are also at risk of being infected with Salmonella and L. monocytogenes if the food is not handled carefully or if their dog licks their skin after eating, so thorough handwashing is important before and after preparing a meal. If you plan to feed your Sheltie a raw diet, consult with your vet to make sure you approach it safely, and watch your Sheltie for signs of illness or digestive issues.

Most homemade diets involve cooking the ingredients, and any recipes you use must come from a reliable source. Your vet or nutrition consultant should be able to provide you with some suggestions. Once you have the recipes, you will need to follow them exactly because substituting ingredients or changing the cooking method will change the nutritional composition of the meal. Also, make sure you only use safe, high-quality ingredients. You can refer to Chapter Three for a list of foods that can be poisonous for dogs.

Let's take a look at the basic nutrients your Sheltie needs:

1. **Protein:** Protein is composed of amino acids, which assist in the growth and repair of cells and, by extension, the tissues and organs formed by these cells. As a result, eating enough protein is vital for your dog's body to function properly. Meat and other animal products, such as cooked eggs, should make up at least half of your Sheltie's diet.

2. **Fats:** Healthy fats provide energy and assist in the absorption of vitamins. Your Sheltie can receive fat from the meat he eats, but be careful not to use meat with a high fat percentage because too much fat can lead to obesity. Omega-3 fatty acids from fish are beneficial in regulating the immune system and reducing inflammation; however, do not rely too heavily on fish as a source of protein or fat. You should only give your dog around one ounce of fish per pound of other meat.

3. **Carbohydrates:** The necessity of carbohydrates in a dog's diet is controversial. Dogs can absorb all the energy they need from protein and fats, so carbs are not necessarily required. However, they can assist in intestine health and supplying glucose to the brain, in addition to providing energy. For dogs that are extremely active or are underweight, car-

bohydrates can also help keep weight on their body. Carbohydrates can be provided by whole grains, such as brown rice or quinoa, and starchy vegetables, such as pureed pumpkin or sweet potatoes.

4. **Vitamins:** Your Sheltie needs to eat enough sources of vitamins A, B, C, D, E, and K. These vitamins help promote a healthy immune system, healthy skin and eyes, and the overall functioning of the body. Many of these vitamins can be found in meat, especially organ meat such as beef liver. Fruits and vegetables can also be a good source of vitamins, fiber, and antioxidants.

5. **Minerals:** Minerals, such as calcium and iron, make up less than one percent of a dog's body weight but are essential for healthy bones and teeth. Many minerals can be found in meat and dairy products, including fresh bones. Plain yogurt can be a good source of calcium, but you should avoid giving your Sheltie cheese because of its high fat content.

SHELTIES ON SOCIAL MEDIA
Sheltie Sandwich

Sheltie Sandwich (@sheltiesandwich) is an Instagram account for two Shelties named Sokka and Lulu. This adorable duo is based in the Netherlands, and with over 24,000 followers is one of the most popular Sheltie Instagram accounts.

When exclusively fed a homemade diet, dogs can often experience nutritional deficiencies, so if this is the route you choose, you will likely need to supplement this diet with certain vitamins and minerals.

Calcium supplementation is generally required with homemade diets. Other nutrients, such as vitamin D, vitamin E, and iodine, may also be lacking. Consult with your nutrition expert to examine any deficiencies in your Sheltie's diet and determine the best method for filling in any gaps. Also, keep in mind that puppies need more nutrients in their diet than adult dogs, so you will need to adjust the amount of food and supplements you provide depending on the age of your Sheltie.

With proper guidance and supplementation, you can provide your Sheltie with a healthy homemade diet. However, keep in mind that not all Shelties will be able to digest these foods well, so depending on how sensitive your pup's stomach is, a homemade diet might not be a viable option. You also might have to adjust the types of foods you offer your pup to accommodate any digestive difficulties.

*Photo Courtesy
of Kathy Ross*

Treats and People Food

Choosing the right treats for your Sheltie is in many ways just as important as choosing the right food. After all, treats are an invaluable training tool, and you're going to end up feeding your puppy a lot of treats while he learns to obey the house rules. If the treats are too calorically dense or contain unhealthy ingredients, this may end up becoming a problem. Just like with regular food, you want to make sure the treats are made with natural whole foods, are free of artificial flavors or preservatives, and are primarily made with protein, vegetables, and fruits rather than grains. For training, you will want to use small, low-calorie treats, but they also need to be enticing enough to encourage your puppy to listen and obey.

Some people also use small pieces of chicken or baby carrots as healthy treats. While this may work well for some Shelties, it won't work for others and should only be given in moderation. Once again, Shelties often have sensitive stomachs, so eating too much people food can upset their bellies. This is important to remember any time you're tempted to feed your Sheltie table scraps—he might love you for it in the moment, but you both might pay for it later.

Feeding your dog people food, especially scraps from the table, also encourages begging. Shelties are creatures of habit, so once the precedent has been set that you will share some of your food, your Sheltie will expect it every time you cook or eat. This will lead to a lot of whining and longing stares, as well as your Sheltie being underfoot while you cook, intently staring at the floor...just in case something falls. The best way to prevent begging is to not give your dog people food in the first place, so your Sheltie learns that this food is for you, not for him.

Weight Management

"Please don't overfeed your Sheltie. Shelties will always make you think they are starving, but don't fall for it. No matter what you feed, be specific about the amount. An average size sheltie that weighs 25 lbs should have about 1-1/2 cups of food per day, depending on their exercise schedule."

SHERRY DEEDS
BellaRose Shelties

The exact amount of food your Sheltie needs will depend on his size and level of activity. Shelties tend to require a higher caloric intake than some dogs their size due to their playful and active nature, but you should always check with your vet to determine your Sheltie's individual needs. Also, keep in mind that puppies will have different nutritional needs than adult dogs. Puppies tend to eat three to four small meals a day, and their food should be specially designed for puppies. After all, puppies need more nutrient-dense food to support their growing bodies, so their food needs to contain higher

Photo Courtesy of Gaby Garcia

levels of protein and fat. You can begin transitioning to feeding adult dog food twice a day between the ages of seven to nine months, but if in doubt, it's better to feed your Sheltie puppy food too long than not long enough. By one year, however, your Sheltie should only eat adult food. Because of the high caloric content, adult dogs can easily become overweight if they are fed puppy food after they are fully grown.

Signs your Sheltie is starting to become overweight include a sagging belly, which is losing its defined angular shape, and not being able to easily feel his ribcage with your fingers. You may start to notice that your Sheltie doesn't have as much stamina as usual and becomes out of breath easily. You can always ask your vet if he or she has any concerns regarding your Sheltie's weight. Remember that Shelties typically weigh 15-25 pounds, but the ideal weight will vary depending on the height and sex of the individual dog.

For example, Winnie was the runt of her litter, so she's on the smaller side of the scale, weighing sixteen pounds. If she were to weigh twenty-five pounds, she would likely be considered obese, but for a larger Sheltie, this might be an ideal weight.

Obesity greatly decreases the overall quality of life for a dog. It increases the risk of numerous health problems, including diabetes, cancer, kidney failure, heart disease, and various skin conditions. The extra weight worsens the effects of any orthopedic conditions, such as hip dysplasia and arthritis, which Shelties are prone to develop as they age. Obesity can also impair the dog's immune system. Even short periods of obesity can cause long-term damage to the dog's body, so if you start to notice your Sheltie gaining too much weight, you need to take immediate steps to help him lose the extra pounds.

If your Sheltie becomes overweight, you will need to speak with your vet to develop a healthy weight-loss plan. You will likely need to reduce the amount of food you give him, but you still need to ensure he's getting enough nutrition. This may involve changing the type of food you buy or reducing the number of treats you give him. You should also start slowly increasing your Sheltie's daily exercise. Keep in mind that his stamina is likely lower right now, so be careful not to push him beyond his capabilities. Instead, slowly build his endurance level back up by developing a daily routine and gradually increasing the length of your walks and other activities when your Sheltie is ready.

Making sure your Sheltie receives a nutritious diet and maintains his recommended weight will ensure that your furry friend will live a long and happy life.

CHAPTER TWELVE
Grooming Your Sheltie

"If something stressful occurs such as a nail trim or bath, Shelties typically are calm and well behaved, but immediately afterwards they will celebrate. They pounce and zoom and roll like they just cheated death."

LINNEA GULSTAD
Sunny Shelties

Photo Courtesy
of Shelly DeViller

Shelties are known for their long, beautiful fur, but what some people don't realize is that they actually have two coats of fur, not just one. The outer layer consists of the long, straight hair you usually see, but underneath there is an undercoat that is much shorter and fluffier. This undercoat is extremely dense

FUN FACT
Lord Scott

Lord Scott was the first Shetland sheep-dog to be registered with the American Kennel Club in 1911. Scott was born in Shetland and imported to New York by John G. Sherman.

and insulates the dogs against both heat and cold. Likewise, in addition to giving Shelties their beautifully distinctive look, the outercoat protects them from the sun's harmful rays.

The undercoat generally sheds more than the outercoat. While you'll likely find plenty of long Sheltie hairs lying around, the tuffs of fluff from the undercoat are what will cover your carpets, furniture, and clothes during shedding season. Shelties shed most heavily in the spring to get rid of the extra insulation which kept them warm during the winter; this shedding prepares them for the warmer summer months. Due to hormonal differences, male Shelties typically shed less than females, and spaying or neutering reduces shedding for both genders. Unspayed females will also shed heavily after every heat cycle, which occurs every six to eight months on average. Still, with either gender, Shelties do shed quite a bit, so you will need to groom your Sheltie regularly to not only keep his coat healthy and beautiful but also keep your home cleaner.

Before we discuss the details of grooming a Sheltie, I want to stress that you should NEVER shave a Shetland Sheepdog. Some people have their Shelties shaved because they think it will help keep their dogs cooler in the summer and reduce shedding. However, because of the way a Sheltie's double coat functions, this ends up having the opposite effect. Shaving a Sheltie actually takes away his protection from the heat rather than making him cooler, which can be dangerous for his health. Although the fur will grow back eventually, shaving it can cause permanent damage to the coat, thinning it and reducing its long-term effectiveness. Also, even if you shave your Sheltie, he will still shed, so there is no benefit to be gained. The only exception would be if your vet says shaving is necessary due to severe skin problems, in which case you would need to carefully follow your vet's instructions to protect your Sheltie's health, but this is a rare situation.

Brushing and Tidying the Coat

"Always brush your dogs coat by mist spraying while brushing. Use a good Brush (Mason Pearson is fantastic) as well as a Pin Brush and slicker brush. Teach your dog to lie down while grooming and do one side at a time. Try to do this once a week if possible. Your dog will be healthier and you will be happier!"

SUZI BEACHAM
Shalamar Shelties

Ideally, you should brush your Sheltie on a weekly basis. Some people even suggest doing a quick brushing every day to remove any dirt and prevent tangles from forming, then complete a more thorough brushing once a week. Regular brushing will not only keep your Sheltie's coat healthy but also promote skin health and proper circulation.

Photo Courtesy of Nadine Shortland

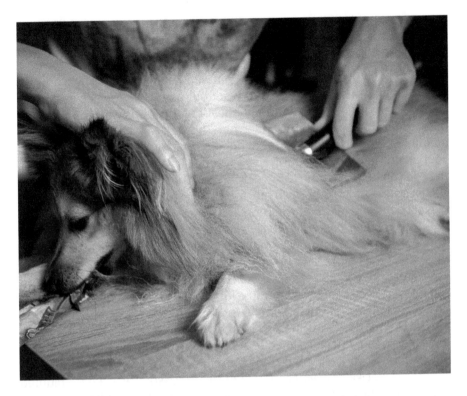

There are several types of brushes you can use, and each one serves a different purpose:

1. **Slicker brush:** A slicker brush will help remove dirt and tangles from the fur and is designed to redistribute the nature oils produced by the Sheltie's body, which will help keep the outercoat shiny and healthy.

2. **Pin brush:** A pin brush has long pins that will help penetrate the layers of the Sheltie's fur and remove any mats and tangles. Just be careful not to push down too hard, or else these pins can poke into the Sheltie, causing pain and distress.

3. **Fine-toothed comb:** A small fine-toothed comb can help remove tangles from sensitive areas, like behind the ears and the feathers behind the legs.

4. **De-shedding tool:** A de-shedding tool, such as a FURminator, is specifically designed to target the undercoat, removing excess fluff and thereby reducing shedding. This can be extremely beneficial, especially during shedding season. However, it is not intended to remove tangles and should not be used on a daily basis, or it can start to remove healthy fur instead of just the dead, excess fur. You also should not press down too

hard with this tool because it could cut your Sheltie's skin, and it should not be used on sensitive areas, like behind the ears. The de-shedding tool can be extremely useful but needs to be used properly.

Start by lightly misting your dog's coat with water, which will help prevent breakage, then use a pin brush to work out any initial tangles in the fur. Don't forget to gently brush through the fur of the tail as well. Next, use the de-shedding tool to target the undercoat. This step will likely take the longest amount of time, especially if it's shedding season or if you haven't groomed your Sheltie in a while. You will end up with piles of wooly fluff—sometimes the pile can be almost the same size as your Sheltie, and you'll wonder how such a little dog could have so much fur! You will likely need to part the fur into sections and tackle one section at a time.

Once you feel like you've finally gotten out all the extra fluff, you can use the fine-toothed comb to work out any hidden tangles, particularly behind the ears, in the feathery fur behind the legs, and under the belly. These sensitive areas are particularly susceptible to building up knots and mats, which can become sore and uncomfortable for your Sheltie if left untreated. It can be helpful to use a detangling spray, and for particularly stubborn mats, you might want to consider using a special de-matting comb as well. De-matting tools have sharp ends designed to cut through mats while they're combed, but of course, you will need to be extremely careful not to cut into your Sheltie's skin. Likewise, you can use pet safety scissors, which have blunted tips, to cut out large mats, but use extreme caution. It can be helpful to hold the scissors close to the dog's skin then cut outwards, rather than cutting into the fur directly. Scissors can easily cut the skin as well as the fur, especially if the dog jumps or moves suddenly, so it's best to try other methods of removing mats first and only use scissors as a last resort.

Finally, use the slicker brush to remove any remaining extra hair from the outercoat, redistribute oils to make the coat shiny and healthy, and stimulate the skin to promote proper circulation.

After you're done brushing your Sheltie, you can use the pet safety scissors to tidy up his coat. It is especially important to trim the fur around the paws and the bottom of the pads. This fur can easily collect mud and gravel, which can impede your Sheltie's ability to walk if left unmanaged. You can do this by holding the scissors flat against the bottom of his paws to trim any straggly hairs until they're flush with the pads, being careful not to angle the scissors inward, then shape the fur around the paws into an oval. The fur on your dog's rear end, under the tail, should also be kept short and tidy to prevent it from becoming dirty with fecal matter. You can also trim any other sections of the fur that are getting unruly, but this is optional. Personally, I'm not comfortable cutting Winnie's fur myself, so I prefer to leave it to the professionals.

Bathing and Drying the Coat

"Always brush your sheltie with a pin brush prior to bathing to release any loose hair or undercoat. It makes it much easier to bath, & much less tangling when you are done. You are also able to reach the skin & give it a good scrub."

SHERRY DEEDS
BellaRose Shelties

Shelties are generally clean dogs and do not need to be bathed very often. In between baths, Shelties will use their tongues to groom themselves, licking their paw and rubbing it on their face like a cat. The necessary bathing frequency for your Sheltie will depend on his environment and activities. Use your judgment to determine when he seems dirty or starts to get smelly; however, you should be fine bathing him once a month or every other month.

Brush your Sheltie before you bathe him as any tangles will be harder to get out of his fur once it is wet. After you finish brushing him, fill the tub with a couple inches of lukewarm water and stand him in the water. Use the shower nozzle or a cup to soak his fur with the water, avoiding his eyes and ears. It can be helpful to place cotton balls in your Sheltie's ears ahead of time to prevent any water or soap from getting inside them, but if you choose to skip this step, just be more careful when you wash around this area. You will also need to place the shower nozzle close to your Sheltie's skin, or else it won't be able to permeate his waterproof outercoat.

It isn't until you see your Sheltie soaking wet that you will realize just how fluffy he really is. Don't be surprised if he shrinks down to at least half his usual size!

Once both layers of your Sheltie's coat are completely saturated with water, you can start to massage shampoo into the fur. Make sure you use shampoo designed for dogs or puppies, not people. Human skin has a different pH balance than dog skin, so our shampoos can irritate or even damage their skin. Lather in the shampoo until his entire body is covered in suds, but be extra careful around his ears and face.

Next, rinse out all the shampoo and hold the nozzle close to your Sheltie's skin to make sure you reach both layers of his coat. Use your other hand to help work out all the shampoo and continue until you can't find any trace of suds anywhere on the dog's body.

You can also add a canine moisturizing conditioner to help make the fur less tangled, which will make future brushing easier, but this step is optional. Some moisturizers need to be rinsed out while others can be left in, so make sure you follow the directions on the bottle.

After the bath, you can wrap your Sheltie in a towel and try to soak up any excess water, then use a blow dryer on low heat to dry him more thoroughly. Be careful not hold it too close to his skin to avoid burning him. Using a blow dryer instead of a towel for most of the drying process will help reduce mats and tangles in the fur. Winnie is terrified of the blow dryer, however, so we usually just dry her with a towel. Then, she likes to run around franticly and roll on the carpet to dry herself.

You will likely need to brush your Sheltie's fur again after the bath to remove any additional loose hairs, but it should be much quicker this time. Then voilà! You have a squeaky-clean Sheltie.

Trimming the Nails

"Keep the nails short and the hair on the bottom of the feet trimmed. I hate to see a Sheltie with long nails and pads full of hair."

ROSE MARIE DORAN
Granite Gables Shetland Sheepdogs

Trimming your Sheltie's nails can seem scary at first, for both you and your puppy. However, it is an important part of the grooming process. If your Sheltie's nails grow too long, they will be forced back up into the nail bed when he walks, which will put pressure on the joints or force the toes to twist sideways. This will cause extreme pain for your Sheltie, and he might even develop arthritis as a result.

Although it's necessary, most dogs don't like having their nails cut. To make the process easier for your Sheltie, it's helpful to get your puppy used to having his paws handled from day one and gradually introduce the nail clippers to your puppy. First, simply let him sniff them, then touch them to his paws without cutting the nails and let him hear the sound, then finally, cut one nail at a time over the course of a few days. You should give your puppy a treat and praise him after each step. Your Sheltie may never enjoy the process, but hopefully, he'll at least be able to tolerate it rather than being terrified.

"Keep nails trimmed! Untrimmed nails can result in early arthritis due to the creation of incorrect pressure points on the foot's skeleton."

LAURA WILLSON
Wildwest Shelties

Cutting your dog's nails can also be a daunting task for you because you don't want to accidentally hurt your Sheltie, and a certain degree of caution is justifiable. If you cut too high up on the nail, you will cut a section called the quick, which contains blood and nerve endings. When this happens, it is extremely painful for the dog and will cause him to bleed, which will likely make him more scared of nail trimming in the future. However, if you're careful and cut only a little bit of the nail at a time, you should be safe.

There are two main types of nail clippers: guillotine and scissors. Some guillotine-style clippers have technology that helps you detect where the quick begins, which helps you cut the nail more safely. However, some people argue that guillotine clippers crush the toe too much, which also hurts the dog. If you have concerns, you can talk to your vet or groomer and see what they recommend.

To trim the nails, hold your dog's paw firmly but gently. Next, cut the hooked tip of the nail at a 45-degree angle, taking off small amounts of the nail at a time. You should only take off the hooked portion of the nail. Stop if you see a circle of white, pink, or grey inside the nail, and do not cut if the nail feels spongy since this indicates you're about to cut the quick. It can be easier to tell where the quick is in light-colored nails because you can see the pink section within the nail. If your Sheltie has a light-colored nail, do this nail first and use it as a guide for the other nails. Don't forget to also trim the dewclaws, located in the interior of the front legs. If the dewclaws aren't trimmed, they'll eventually curve around and stab into your Sheltie's legs.

If you do accidentally cut the quick, don't panic. Panicking will only make your Sheltie more afraid than he already is. Instead, quickly compress the nail with a paper towel to stop the bleeding. Hold it there for a couple minutes. If the bleeding doesn't stop, you can try adding ice to reduce the blood flow. Styptic powder is also very effective at stopping the bleeding and can be purchased at most pet stores, or some people suggest using corn starch as an alternative home remedy. Put the powder in a small bowl or the palm of your hand and dip the nail into it. Styptic powder can sting at first, so you'll have to hold the paw steady in case your Sheltie jumps back. Continue until the bleeding stops, then try to keep your Sheltie off his feet for at least half an hour. Make sure you reward him for how brave he is and try to minimize the fear associated with nail clipping in the future.

Cleaning Ears, Eyes, and Teeth

EARS

If your Sheltie's ears are clean and pink on the inside, as well as odorless, you likely do not need to use a cleaning solution. Cleaning your dog's ears too often can actually cause irritation and infection, so you should hold off unless you notice signs of irritation, such as a mild odor or your Sheltie shaking or scratching his head excessively. Call your vet if you notice any redness and inflammation, a foul or yeasty odor, or pain, as these symptoms can indicate a more serious issue. Trying to clean an infected ear yourself can exacerbate the problem, so be sure to follow any instructions your vet gives you.

For more basic care, you can use a high-quality dog ear cleaner at home. Avoid any that contain hydrogen peroxide or alcohol, as these can irritate the ear canal. Likewise, do not try using hydrogen peroxide as a home remedy; instead, ask your vet what ear cleaner would work best for your Sheltie. To clean the ear:

1. Position your Sheltie on the floor in front of you, sitting between your legs. If possible, I would recommend having a second person hold your Sheltie during the cleaning process; trying to do it by yourself is doable but difficult because your Sheltie will likely squirm and try to run away.

2. Hold the ear up to expose the ear canal and move any long hairs out of the way. Hold the cleaning solution in your other hand.

3. Without touching the ear with the tip of the bottle, squeeze the cleaning solution into the ear, filling the ear canal.

4. Still holding the ear up with one hand, gently massage the base of the ear with your other hand to help work the cleaning solution into any debris stuck in the ear canal. You should hear a swishing sound.

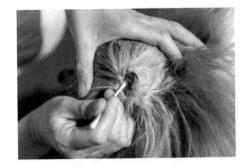

5. Gently wipe the inside of the ear with a cotton ball. Do not go deeper into the ear canal than the depth of one knuckle and never insert a Q-tip into the ear canal, as this can damage the dog's ear drum.

6. Allow your Sheltie to shake his head, then hold the ear and wipe the inside with a cotton ball again to remove any remaining debris or cleaning solution. You might also need a towel to clean up any solution that gets on the dog's face or on you.

Your Sheltie will likely not be very happy with you during this process, but if he appears to be in any pain, stop immediately and speak with your vet before proceeding.

EYES

Like humans, it is not uncommon for dogs to have "eye gunk," a small amount of gooey discharge in the corner of their eyes. If this discharge is clear and your Sheltie is not exhibiting any other signs of irritation or infection, you have nothing to worry about. Simply take a wet washcloth or paper towel and wipe it away. It is important to not let the discharge build up, however, because it will eventually harden and become crusty, which could hurt your Sheltie's eyes and could possibly become infected. If you notice this discharge changes color or consistency, your Sheltie's eyes become discolored, or he appears to have difficulty seeing or starts pawing at his eyes, talk to your vet. Your Sheltie may have an underlying condition or infection, and you might need to apply ointment or eye drops. Your vet will be able to give you instructions on how to proceed.

Shelties are not as prone to developing tear stains as breeds with shorter noses, but they can still get these marks, especially if they have light-colored fur around their eyes. Tears stains are dark marks under the eyes caused by excessively watery eyes. If your Sheltie develops these marks, you can wipe around his eyes with a cloth using a pet-safe eye rinse to reduce the appearance. If tear stains become a consistent problem, you should consider improving the quality of your Sheltie's food, making sure it's made with natural whole foods, and providing clean, filtered water. Any artificial additives and preservatives in dog food, as well as the impurities in tap water, can contribute to tear stains. If your Sheltie exhibits any signs of irritation, or if you notice that your dog only gets tear stains in one eye, which can be a sign of a blocked tear duct, you should talk to your vet.

TEETH

Taking proper care of your Sheltie's teeth will not only help minimize bad breath but also prevent tooth decay and gum disease. While some treats advertise their ability to keep teeth clean, you will still need to use an actual toothbrush and canine toothpaste; do not use human toothpaste as it is toxic for dogs. Ideally, you should brush your Sheltie's teeth on a daily basis. He likely won't be thrilled about the idea, though, so you will need to introduce the toothbrush slowly. Start by getting your puppy used to having his mouth handled and by letting him sniff the toothbrush without any toothpaste on it. Next, gently touch the toothbrush to the teeth. Once your Sheltie can tolerate this, you can introduce the toothpaste. First, show it to him and let him lick some from your finger. Then, you will be able to put it on the toothbrush and start gently brushing the teeth. Don't forget to brush the sides and backs of the teeth and give your Sheltie lots of praise for his patience.

Professional Grooming

Unless you are proficient with dog grooming tools, you will likely need to take your Sheltie to a professional groomer on a regular basis. The groomer will be able to tidy up your Sheltie's coat, trim his nails, and thoroughly bathe him, which can help supplement your grooming routine at home. Sometimes you can even get a deep-conditioning treatment, which will make the fur feel soft and healthy. Since your Sheltie's long coat can make the summer heat extremely uncomfortable, you can ask for a slightly shorter haircut during these months, but remember to never shave him.

Unless your groomer is familiar with Shelties, you will probably need to give detailed instructions on how you want the fur to be shaped. Most groomers will do a simple "puppy cut," making all the fur the same length, but this takes away from the Sheltie's trademark shape. With Winnie, I don't like when the groomers remove her "mane," the longer fur around her neck and chest, so I simply ask them to trim it a little rather than cutting it down to the length of the other fur.

When choosing a groomer, keep in mind not only your budget, but also the cleanliness of the facility and the way the employees treat your dog. You will be trusting your Sheltie with these people for a couple of hours, so you want to feel confident they will not mistreat or be too rough with your fur baby when you're not around. Reading reviews of other people's experiences online can also aid you in your decision.

Overall, Shetland Sheepdogs are not low-maintenance dogs. Properly grooming your Sheltie will require a lot of time and effort, but the end result will be a healthy dog with a gorgeous coat, which makes it all worthwhile.

CHAPTER THIRTEEN
Sheltie Healthcare

Choosing the right veterinarian is a major decision because this person will play a crucial role in your Sheltie's care. Your vet will be your go-to person whenever your Sheltie has a problem or you have any questions, so you need to be able to trust his or her judgment and advice.

Here are some factors to consider when choosing a veterinarian:

1. **Recommendations:** Ask any friends or family members where they have taken their pets and what their experience was like. They will be able to tell you which vets they loved and which ones to avoid, which should help narrow down your list.

2. **Philosophy:** You want to make sure your vet's philosophy of pet care aligns with your own. For example, if you want a more holistic approach, you should find a vet who encourages dietary and lifestyle changes to address problems rather than immediately resorting to medication.

3. **Cleanliness:** Visit each prospective vet's office to get a feel for the environment before you even bring your puppy home. If an office seems grungy or unkempt, you should go elsewhere for veterinary care. A veterinary office should be as clean and sanitary as a doctor's office.

4. **Location:** You don't want your veterinary office to be too far away from your house in case you have to drive there quickly for an emergency. You should also check what the clinic's policy is for after-hours care if you have an urgent problem in the middle of the night or over the weekend; they should be able to tell you where the nearest 24-hour emergency facility is if necessary.

Photo Courtesy of Andrea Porter

Photo Courtesy of Francine Chenier

5. **Fees:** Ask about standard fees and financial assistance plans. Prices will vary depending on the practice, but remember that when it comes to health care, cheaper isn't always better.

6. **Accreditation and Experience:** Your veterinary office should be accredited by the American Animal Hospital Association (AAHA). It would also be helpful if your vet has experience working with Shetland Sheepdogs.

Ultimately, both you and your Sheltie need to be comfortable with the vet you choose. When you take your Sheltie in for his first vet visit, watch how the staff interacts with him. If at any time you aren't comfortable with what you see or hear, you can always switch to a different practice.

The First Vet Visit

You should schedule your Sheltie's first vet visit before you pick up the puppy to ensure you don't have to wait a month or two before getting an appointment. If you bought the puppy from a breeder, the contract will likely require a veterinary exam within three days of bringing the puppy home, as well as any necessary checkups and vaccinations. Don't forget to bring any relevant paperwork and records from the breeder to your appointment. If you adopted your Sheltie from a shelter, he likely won't have as many medical records, if any, so getting him checked out by a licensed vet as soon as possible is even more important to establish a baseline for his current condition and to discuss any necessary care in the future.

The first vet visit will involve a comprehensive examination of the puppy, including weight, temperature, teeth, ears, eyes, nose, skin and coat, and heart and lung sounds. You will likely need to bring a fecal sample with you, so the vet can check for worms. Some internal parasites are relatively common in puppies, and medication may be required.

If your puppy does require any treatment, make sure you understand the instructions and ask questions if necessary. You will need to follow the directions precisely.

During the first visit, I would also recommend asking about microchipping. This is a minimally invasive procedure involving inserting a microchip between the puppy's shoulder blades. Once you register the microchip, it will contain your contact information. Then, if your Sheltie ever gets lost and someone brings him to a veterinary office or shelter, the workers can scan the microchip and easily contact you to reunite you with your pup. However, keep in mind that unless you register the microchip, the numbers attached to it will be useless. There are several different options for registering your Sheltie's microchip; some registries only accept certain brands of microchip, though, and they may charge an annual or one-time fee. For example, the AKC has a registry that charges a small one-time fee, while the Michelson Found Animals Registry is a nonprofit that offers free registration; both registries accept any brand of microchip. You can ask your vet for recommendations, and you have the option of registering with multiple organizations.

Overall, this first visit offers the opportunity for you to get to know the vet, as well as for the vet to get to know you and your Sheltie. You will discuss your Sheltie's history and any future treatment plans, such as vaccinations and spaying or neutering. You can also ask questions about your puppy's diet, request recommendations for trainers, or bring up any other concerns you might have. Then, you will schedule any necessary follow-up appointments.

Spaying / Neutering Your Sheltie

Unless you are planning to breed your Sheltie, you will likely need to neuter him (or spay for a female). Neutering is the surgical removal of the testicles, and spaying is the removal of the uterus and ovaries. This procedure is highly recommended and is generally considered the responsible choice. Most breeders and shelters require spaying/neutering as a term of adoption. There are several benefits to spaying/neutering your Sheltie:

1. **Reduce the number of unwanted pets.** The United States has a major canine overpopulation problem. Spaying or neutering your Sheltie will help reduce the number of unwanted litters, thereby lessening the number of dogs that end up homeless, in shelters, and/or euthanized.

2. **Reduce health risks.** Removing a dog's reproductive organs greatly reduces the risk of testicular or uterine cancer, as well as mammary gland tumors, which means there will be an increased probability of your Sheltie living a longer and healthier life.

3. **Promote a calmer, gentler disposition.** While Shelties are typically already gentle by nature, intact male dogs are generally more aggressive than their neutered counterparts. Neutering your Sheltie will lower his testosterone levels, thereby reducing or eliminating any typical male dominant behavior, including humping other pets and objects.

Photo Courtesy of Sue Bowen

4. Eliminate problems associated with the heat cycle. Unspayed females will typically go into heat around twice a year, and they will expel a bloody discharge which will stain your carpets and anything else it touches. Both males and females will also roam to find mates, which increases the risk of your Sheltie running away and possibly getting lost or hit by a car.

Still, this procedure is a major operation and does come with some risks. There is the possibility your Sheltie will respond poorly to the anesthesia. Shetland Sheepdogs, among other herding breeds, are prone to having a mutation of the MDR1 (Multi Drug Resistance) gene, which can cause negative and sometimes even fatal reactions to certain drugs, including anesthetics. A DNA test can confirm whether your Sheltie has this mutation. Most vets are aware of this risk with herding dogs, but just in case, you should bring up this concern prior to surgery. Your vet will be able to adjust the pre-op and surgical plan to ensure maximum safety for your Sheltie.

The age at which your Sheltie has this surgery is another major factor to consider. Some shelters and vets have begun spaying/neutering puppies as young as eight weeks old. Performing this procedure early, specifically before the puppy reaches sexual maturity or the first heat cycle, can be beneficial in terms of preventing accidental pregnancies and reducing the risk of cancer. However, studies have shown that spaying/neutering puppies too young can negatively impact their development and cause joint and bone problems later in life. Most people wait until their puppy is six to nine months old before performing this operation, although some recommend waiting an entire year. You should discuss any concerns with your vet and come up with a plan that will best benefit your Sheltie's long-term health.

The cost of spaying or neutering a puppy can range from around $35-300 depending on where you live and where you go for the procedure. Humane Societies and low-cost clinics typically charge much less than a traditional veterinary office, but you need to make sure the clinic you go to for the procedure is clean and trustworthy. Also, keep in mind the cost of this single operation, while potentially pricey, is still much less than the cost of caring for a pregnant dog and a litter of puppies.

After the surgery, female dogs might need to stay at the veterinary clinic overnight, but male dogs can typically go home the same day. Carefully follow any post-op instructions to ensure proper healing. You will likely need to limit your Sheltie's activity for around seven to ten days, or as long as your vet recommends, and he will need a quiet place away from other animals to rest and recover. He will also likely need to wear a protective cone to prevent him from licking or biting his incisions. Call your vet if you notice any swelling or discharge at the incision site, or if your Sheltie is exhibiting signs of lethargy, decreased appetite, or vomiting.

Vaccinations

Over the first year, your puppy will require several rounds of vaccinations, as well as additional booster shots every year or two for the rest of his life. These vaccines will protect your Sheltie from various diseases, which could be detrimental to his health or possibly even fatal. Here is a recommended timeline for vaccines provided by the AKC[1]:

Age	Recommended Vaccinations	Optional Vaccinations
6-8 weeks	Distemper, parvovirus	Bordetella
10-12 weeks	DHPP (vaccines for distemper, adenovirus [hepatitis], parainfluenza, and parvovirus)	Influenza, Leptospirosis, Bordetella, Lyme disease per lifestyle as recommended by veterinarian
16-18 weeks	DHPP, rabies	Influenza, Lyme disease, Leptospirosis, Bordetella per lifestyle
12-16 months	DHPP, rabies	Coronavirus, Leptospirosis, Bordetella, Lyme disease
Every 1-2 years	DHPP	Influenza, Coronavirus, Leptospirosis, Bordetella, Lyme disease per lifestyle
Every 1-3 years	Rabies (as required by law)	none

Speak to your veterinarian to determine the exact vaccines your puppy will need based on your lifestyle. For example, if you plan to go hiking with your Sheltie where he might be exposed to ticks, the Lyme disease vaccine will be necessary; however, this may not be needed if you're not very outdoorsy and typically stay in the city. Likewise, the Bordetella (kennel cough) vaccine is often required if you plan on boarding your Sheltie, putting him in doggy daycare, or attending group training classes. Ultimately, the goal is

---

1   Chart provided by the American Kennel Club, www.akc.org/expert-advice/health/puppy-shots-complete-guide.

to stop the spread of preventable diseases, so your Sheltie, and any other dogs he might encounter, will stay healthy and live longer. Of course, you're welcome to ask your vet about any questions or concerns you have regarding vaccinations.

Photo Courtesy
of Yvonne Lamon

Annual Vet Visit

Ideally, you should take your Sheltie to the vet for a check-up at least once a year. Like your first appointment, the annual vet visit will involve a holistic look at your Sheltie's health, including weight, heart and lung sounds, coat and skin, eyes and ears, and dental health. During these checkups, you will also have the opportunity to bring up any questions or concerns you have about your pup. The goal of these appointments is to be proactive and take preventive steps for your Sheltie's health instead of waiting for problems to develop.

FUN FACT
Ch. Halstor's Peter Pumpkin, ROM

The Shetland sheepdog who sired the greatest number of champion dogs was Ch. Halstor's Peter Pumpkin, ROM. ROM stands for Register of Merit and is a title given to dogs who have produced champions. This prolific Sheltie was born on July 13, 1965, bred by Edith Overly, and sired 106 champion dogs.

Common Diseases and Conditions in Shelties

When bred carefully, Shelties are generally healthy dogs, but this does not mean they will be free of any medical problems. The following outlines some of the conditions Shetland Sheepdogs are prone to develop. Although the correlation of the prevalence of these conditions within the breed has been observed, this does not mean these conditions are common or that there is a high likelihood of your Sheltie developing them. Dogs with known health problems are generally not bred, but you should ask the breeder about your puppy's family medical history to be aware of any additional genetic predisposition. This list is meant to inform you of potential symptoms to watch for, so if your Sheltie starts to show signs of one of these conditions, you can go to your vet for treatment before the condition worsens.

Hip Dysplasia: Hip dysplasia involves the subluxation of the hip joint, which damages the joint and can eventually lead to arthritis. This condition is most commonly found in larger breeds, but some smaller purebreds are also at risk, including Shelties. Symptoms typically show up around middle-age but can start younger. Obesity can also increase the risk of developing this condition due to the added pressure on the joints. Talk to your vet if you notice your Sheltie limping and avoiding putting pressure on a hind leg, hesitating when walking upstairs, or hopping like a bunny when running. Your vet will need to conduct a physical examination and perform x-rays for an official diagnosis. Treatment includes lifestyle changes such as weight management, switching to low-impact exercises, and massage therapy, but surgery may also be considered in more severe cases.

Patellar Luxation: Patellar luxation is another joint problem, but this one is more common in small breeds. It involves the kneecap shifting out of position, causing pain and difficulty walking. Once again, this condition typically shows up around middle-age but can be seen earlier, and obesity will worsen its effects. With patellar luxation, your Sheltie will limp and hold up his paw, avoiding putting pressure on his leg. This can last anywhere from ten minutes to a couple of days, and it can be a recurring issue. Your vet will need to examine your Sheltie's legs and take x-rays to diagnose this condition. Your vet can teach you how to help massage the kneecap back into place. More severe cases may also require corrective surgery.

Dermatomyositis: Dermatomyositis, also known as Collie Nose or Sheltie Skin Syndrome, is a skin condition most prevalent in herding breeds. It typically shows up in puppies and can start as early as seven weeks of age.

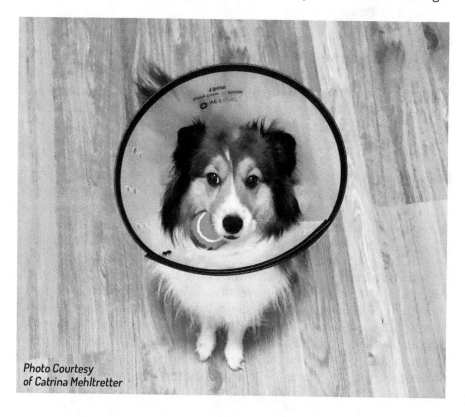

Photo Courtesy of Catrina Mehltretter

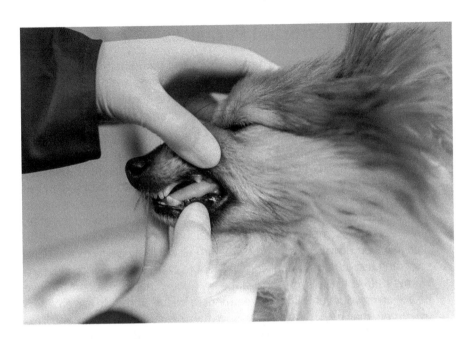

Adult-onset dermatomyositis is rare but possible. Symptoms include skin lesions, scaling, crusting, hair loss, and redness and inflammation on the face. Exposure to UV light can aggravate these symptoms. Treatment options include antibiotics, steroid creams, and sometimes even tattooing black ink on the affected area to help protect it from UV light. Switching to hypoallergenic shampoos and implementing dietary changes can sometimes help as well. These treatments will not completely cure this condition, however, only manage the symptoms. In extremely severe cases, hospitalization may be required, and sometimes euthanasia is the most humane option.

Scleral Ectasia: Scleral ectasia, or Collie eye anomaly as it is more commonly called, is a genetic condition that affects eye development in the womb. With Collie eye, the choroid, which supports the retina, can be underdeveloped, and sometimes the retina can be detached, resulting in impaired vision. There is no treatment for this condition, but dogs who have it are not bred, which reduces its prevalence.

Von Willebrand's Disease: Von Willebrand's Disease (VWD) is a bleeding disorder caused by a genetic mutation. Symptoms include a bloody nose, blood in the urine or stool, and bleeding gums. If you suspect your Sheltie has VWD, talk to your vet. It is important to know whether your Sheltie has VWD before performing any operations, including spaying or neutering, because the condition can cause excessive bleeding during surgery, which can lead to death. There is no cure, but extra precautions may be taken, including medications to help promote blood clotting.

Internal and External Parasites

In addition to these common health conditions, your Sheltie may become infected by parasites at some point in his life. Parasites are organisms that live in or on another living creature and feed on the host.

The following list includes some of the common internal parasites you might encounter:

1. **Heartworms:** Dogs can get heartworms if they are bitten by an infected mosquito. The heartworms enter the bloodstream and travel to the heart and lungs where they damage and clog the blood vessels as they grow, resulting in severe heart and lung disease and eventually total heart failure. An infected dog may have a cough, tire easily, or have a reduced appetite; however, these symptoms will not appear until the heartworms have already slowed down the blood flow. Your vet will likely perform a routine screening test at your annual appointment to catch the presence of heartworms before these symptoms appear. If your Sheltie is found to have heartworms, your vet will begin treatment to kill the worms. In extreme cases, surgery may be necessary to remove them. Heartworm treatment is expensive and risky, though, so preventative care should be prioritized. Your vet can provide you with options for preventive treatment that will protect your Sheltie from these harmful worms; you will just need to remember to administer the treatment at the prescribed intervals.

   NOTE: The MDR1 gene mutation, which is prevalent in herding breeds, can cause a severe, life-threatening reaction to ivermectin, the active ingredient in many heartworm prevention medications. Signs of ivermectin toxicity include lethargy, disorientation, loss of appetite, inability to stand, tremors or seizures, slow heartbeat, difficulty breathing, and sudden blindness. Call your vet immediately if you notice any of these symptoms, and if you know your Sheltie has this mutation, make sure any heartworm medication you use does not include this ingredient.

2. **Roundworms:** Roundworms are a common parasite typically seen in puppies. Symptoms include diarrhea, vomiting, cough, and malnourishment. Your vet will examine your puppy's stool sample to look for evidence of roundworms and will prescribe medication if necessary.

3. **Ringworm:** Despite the name, ringworm is a type of fungus, not a worm. Ringworm causes lesions on the head, ears, paws, and forelimbs, which often cause circular bald spots and can be red in the center. Puppies are more likely to become infected than adults, but adult dogs with weakened immune systems are also at risk. Treatment options include medicated shampoo, ointments, or oral medications.

4. **Hookworm:** Hookworm larvae live in soil, so dogs can become infected by ingesting dirt, sometimes through routine self-cleaning. The hookworm then attaches itself to the intestinal wall and feeds on the dog's blood, which causes diarrhea and weight loss. Puppies typically have a more severe reaction to the blood loss than adults. Your vet can detect the presence of hookworm by examining a stool sample and will prescribe medication if necessary.

5. **Tapeworms:** Dogs can become infected by ingesting a host organism that has a tapeworm egg, such as a flea. Once ingested, the egg will settle into the dog's intestines and grow to maturity. As the tapeworm grows, segments will break off and can be found in the dog's stool. These segments look like grains of rice. Your vet will examine your Sheltie's stool sample to make a diagnosis. Tapeworms typically cause diarrhea and weight loss, and treatment options include oral medication and injections.

6. **Whipworms:** Whipworms are small worms that live in the large intestine. Dogs can become infected by sniffing or licking ground that has been contaminated by whipworm. Signs of infection include watery or bloody diarrhea and weight loss. The dog's stool may also have a mucus covering. If your Sheltie is exhibiting signs of whipworm infection, your vet will likely prescribe a deworming medication.

These little pests aren't the only things vying to feed off your Sheltie, however. While internal parasites live and mature inside the host's body, external parasites attach themselves to the outside of the host organism, i.e., your dog. Here we will outline some of the most common external parasites.

FLEAS

These tiny wingless insects feed on mammals, including dogs, and their bites cause itchiness and irritation. You might not notice your Sheltie has fleas unless he starts scratching himself incessantly or unless you part his fur and look for signs of their existence. Since Shelties have such long fur, you might not be able to find any live fleas, but you should be able to see their waste. Fleas digest the dog's blood and leave behind tiny black specks that look like poppy seeds or dirt. You can test to see if it's "flea dirt" by dabbing it with a damp tissue or paper towel. If it is flea dirt, it will start to turn red as the water rehydrates the blood. If you discover that your Sheltie has fleas, you will need to act quickly to get rid of them before your entire house becomes infested.

Your Sheltie can bring eggs into any room, then the flea pupae can burrow deep into your carpet or furniture where they will remain safe until they hatch into adults. To get rid of fleas, you will need to administer a product to your Sheltie that is designed to kill adult fleas and eggs, in addition to regularly vacuuming and washing his bedding. This process can take a few months, but once the flea pupae develop into adults, they will be attracted to your Sheltie and jump onto him. Then the flea treatment will kill them. However, I would highly recommend that you apply preventative flea treatment to stop fleas before they become a problem in the first place.

There are three main options for flea treatment:

1. **Flea collars:** While in the past, flea collars were largely ineffective, newer models have been shown to prevent flea infestations safely and effectively. However, these collars typically leave a chemical residue on the dog and the surrounding environment, so this may not be a safe option for homes with young children.

2. **Topical treatments:** Topical treatments are medications applied directly to the dog's skin and can be effective in preventing a variety of parasites, including fleas and ticks. However, to avoid potential poisoning, the dog should not be allowed to lick the application site and should be kept away from children and other pets until the medication has completely dried or been absorbed into the skin. You should also speak to your vet before using any topical flea treatments if you have a cat since these treatments often contain ingredients that are toxic for felines.

3. **Oral medications:** Oral medications can also prevent a variety of parasites, including fleas, ticks, and heartworms, and they come in pill and chewable forms. Oral medications are typically the safest option for households with children or other pets that might come in contact with any external chemicals.

Your vet will help you choose the right flea treatment based on your Sheltie's age and environmental factors.

TICKS

If you spend time outdoors with your Sheltie, especially in the woods or in fields of long grass, he might end up getting a tick. Ticks can cause serious illnesses such as Lyme disease, so it is important to check your Sheltie after being in an at-risk environment and remove any ticks as soon as possible.

To check for ticks, run your fingers all over your Sheltie's body to feel for bumps. If you feel a bump, check to see what color it is. If it's black, brown, or tan, it might be a tick. If it's the same color as your Sheltie's skin, it might just be a clogged pore known as a sebaceous cyst. Sebaceous cysts are basically pimples and are usually harmless, but check with your vet any time you find an unusual mass on your Sheltie's body just to be safe.

If you find a tick, do not try to remove it with your fingers, and do not try to kill it with Vaseline, repellents, or a hot match. Instead, use a pair of tweezers or a tick removal tool to get as close to your Sheltie's skin as possible and get a firm grip on the tick. Be careful not to crush it. Slowly and steadily pull upwards to remove the tick. Once the tick is removed, do not put it in the trash or sink; it can crawl back out. Instead, put it in isopropyl alcohol to kill it, and place the tick in a sealed plastic bag. You may want to save it to show your vet, or you can simply take a picture of the tick for identification and dispose of it. Next, wash your hands thoroughly, clean the area on your Sheltie's skin with an antiseptic, and disinfect the tweezers with alcohol.

Watch your Sheltie closely over the next couple weeks. If you notice any signs of lethargy, loss of appetite, swollenness, or any other unusual symptoms, call your vet. Your Sheltie might need to be tested and treated for tick-borne diseases. Once again, applying preventative treatment ahead of time would be preferable to dealing with a tick.

MITES AND LICES

Mites and lice can both cause extreme itching and irritation, as well as potential hair loss and infection. Since they are microscopic, they need to be diagnosed by a skin scraping at the veterinary office. Keep in mind that canine lice and human lice are different, so the lice found on your dog will not be transferred to you or your family. However, mites can sometimes cause itchy red spots on humans.

It is important to be vigilant in watching your Sheltie for any unusual behaviors or symptoms and to call your vet if you have any concerns. After all, your Sheltie can't tell you when he doesn't feel good, so his actions speak for him. As a pet parent, it's your job to ensure his health and well-being by providing any necessary preventative treatment and noticing when something seems wrong. With the right care, your Sheltie will be able to live a long, healthy, and happy life.

CHAPTER FOURTEEN
Traveling With Your Sheltie

At some point, you will need to travel with your Sheltie, whether you are moving across the country or just driving to the veterinary office. You need to make sure that your Sheltie remains safe during these trips, as well as when you can't take him with you.

Before traveling anywhere with your Sheltie, you should make sure he is well-trained and socialized. People are generally much more willing to accommodate a friendly, well-mannered dog than a dog that is constantly barking and causing trouble. You should also crate-train your Sheltie as soon as possible since this will be necessary for driving, flying, or staying in a hotel. Refer to Chapter Five for instructions on how to crate-train your Sheltie.

If you are crossing any borders or going on an extended trip, you will also need to bring your Sheltie to the vet for a checkup to make sure all his health records and vaccinations are up to date; you will need to bring these records with you on your trip.

Traveling by Car

Just as you wear a seat belt when you drive, you should also make sure your Sheltie is safely secured any time he is in the car. Dogs should never be allowed to roam freely inside the car, and they should never ride in the back of a truck. The safest way for your Sheltie to travel in a car is in a carefully secured crate. Harnesses and restraints can help keep the dog from distracting the driver, but they may not be enough to protect him in a crash. Your Sheltie should also never ride in the front seat, and you should never leave him alone in the car. In the summer, the internal temperature of a car will heat up much faster than the

CELEBRITY SHELTIES

Emu Cyrus

American singer-songwriter Miley Cyrus is a very proud Sheltie owner. Her Sheltie is named Emu Coyne Cyrus and was adopted in 2014. Cyrus was so enamored with her furry companion that she got a tattoo in his likeness in 2017. Emu makes regular appearances on Cyrus's Instagram with the hashtag #emusfanclub.

Photo Courtesy
of Daniel & Bonita VanValkenburgh

external temperature even if the windows are cracked open, and in the winter, the temperature can easily become fatally cold.

    If you're on a long road trip, you should bring someone else with you who can stay with the dog when you go inside any rest areas. You will also need to make plenty of stops to allow your Sheltie to relieve himself and stretch his legs. You should bring water for him, but it might be best to drive when his belly is empty, especially if he is prone to getting car sick. To avoid giving him an upset stomach, you can give him a light meal three to four hours prior to departure.

Flying with Your Sheltie

Before flying with your Sheltie, stop and consider whether the benefits of bringing him with you outweigh the risks. While you might enjoy having your furry friend with you during your weeklong vacation, the temporary enjoyment may not be worth the stress of flying and potential dangers. In general, it's best to avoid flying with dogs unless absolutely necessary.

The size of your Sheltie is an important factor to consider when deciding whether to fly with him because this will determine if he will be allowed to remain in the cabin with you or if he will be placed in a cargo area. Typically, airlines only allow dogs in the cabin if their crate fits under the seat. Check with your desired airline to see the specifications for the crates allowed as carry-ons. Your Sheltie needs to fit comfortably in the crate without touching the sides and must still be able to move around. Most Shelties will be too big to meet these specifications, but if your Sheltie is extremely small, he might qualify. If your Sheltie is small enough to fly in the cabin, he will need to remain in his crate under the seat in front of you for the duration of the flight.

If your Sheltie has to fly cargo, the trip can be risky and very traumatic for him. After all, he'll experience the stress of separation from you while also being exposed to loud, scary noises and being jostled around. Far too many people have also shared horror stories of their pets being injured or even killed in transit. Again, it's best to avoid flying with your dog if at all possible. If you have no alternative option to flying, extensively research the airline policies regarding transporting pets before choosing a flight; some airlines are more accommodating than others.

Other factors to consider include your Sheltie's age and personality. Young puppies are usually not allowed to fly, so review the age requirements for the specific airline. Some Shelties may also be more comfortable with air travel than others. Flying is stressful for any dog, so if your Sheltie is already prone to anxiety, it might end up being a deeply traumatizing experience for him.

However, do NOT give your Sheltie a sedative or tranquilizer before the trip to keep him calm. Tranquilizers suppress the respiratory system, which could make it difficult for him to breathe at such a high altitude. He might also have an adverse reaction to the drug itself. Overall, the risk is not worth the potential benefits.

If you are going to fly with your Sheltie, you will need to call the airline well in advance. Only a certain number of animals are allowed on each flight, and these spots are given on a first-come-first-served basis. It would also be a good idea to call closer to the date of your flight to confirm, so you don't encounter any unexpected surprises when you arrive at the airport.

*Photo Courtesy
of Nadine Shortland*

Carefully review the airline's pet policy prior to the flight and follow these rules precisely. Keep in mind some locations ban pet travel, so make sure your destination is not on this list. The airline will specify what type of carrier you need to use, which you will need to clearly label with your dog's name and your contact information. You will also need to provide health and vaccination certifications in advance, and you will likely need to arrive at the airport early.

You should book a nonstop flight, and if your Sheltie is flying cargo, make sure you are on the same schedule as him. Most airlines will ask you to attach a small bag of food to the top of the carrier in case of any unexpected delays, but you should feed your dog three to four hours before the flight to give his stomach time to settle. You can also attach a bowl to the inside of the crate and fill it with ice. This way, the water will not spill while your dog is being loaded in the plane, but the ice will melt during the flight and provide hydration.

Also, keep in mind the temperature of both your current location and your destination. While the pet cargo area should be temperature controlled, most airlines will not allow you to fly with your pet if the weather outside is either too hot or too cold. If possible, it is best to book an early morning or late evening flight during the summer or a midday flight during the winter.

Once you arrive at your destination, grab any checked baggage and immediately head to the designated location to pick up your Sheltie. You should have a current photo of him on your phone to help the airline workers find him in case he gets lost. Afterwards, take him outside as soon as possible, so he can stretch his legs and relieve himself.

Photo Courtesy of Esther Wijma

Hotel Stays

If you are traveling with your Sheltie, another important consideration is the hotel stay. While many hotels claim to be "pet friendly," not all hotels are equal in this regard. Let's take a look at some factors to consider when choosing a hotel:

1. **Fees:** Many hotels charge an additional fee if you are traveling with your pet, and some require an additional, nonrefundable deposit to cover any potential damages. Some hotels charge a nightly fee, which can add up quickly, while others only require a single payment for the duration of the stay. Carefully review the hotel's policy so you're not hit with any unexpected charges. You can also search for hotels without any additional pet fees, which can be extremely helpful, especially if you're traveling on a budget.

2. **Location:** Many hotel chains are located on busy streets near the highway, which might not be ideal for walking a dog. Make sure there's enough grassy space nearby where it is safe to walk your Sheltie. Getting a room on the ground floor might also be more convenient for bathroom trips outside, but if your Sheltie tends to bark when people walk outside your house, you might want to get a room higher up or at least away from the busy parking lot and sidewalks.

3. **Itinerary:** Check the hotel's policy regarding leaving pets alone in the room. Some hotels are fine with it as long as the dog doesn't bark and stays in a crate when unattended, while others require pets to be supervised at all times. If you cannot leave your Sheltie alone in the hotel room, you will either need to only visit pet-friendly places or plan for someone to watch your dog while you're away. Some hotels offer extra amenities, such as dog walking and pet spas, so be sure to take advantage of these services if you're going to be away from your Sheltie for an extended period of time.

You won't know how your Sheltie will react to staying in a hotel until you try it. However, sticking to your normal routine as much as possible and bringing some familiar items from home, such as his crate, a blanket, and a chew toy, will help ease anxiety and make the trip more enjoyable for both you and your Sheltie.

*Photo Courtesy
of Britt Mertens*

Boarding Kennels and Dog Sitters

If you can't bring your Sheltie with you when you leave town, you will need to make accommodations for him while you're gone. Unless you have a friend or relative who can take care of him for you, you will need to either leave him at a boarding kennel or hire a pet sitter.

If you leave your Sheltie in a boarding kennel, you have the assurance that he will be cared for by professionals, and you don't have to worry about a stranger coming into your home to take care of him. Your Sheltie will also have the opportunity to socialize with different people and animals. However, he might become more stressed being in an unfamiliar environment surrounded by strangers.

If your Sheltie is prone to anxiety or if he typically doesn't interact well with other dogs, a boarding kennel is not your best option. There's also the risk of infectious diseases being spread, such as kennel cough, and sometimes the dogs' food can get mixed up, which might lead to gastrointestinal upset if your pup is fed the wrong food. Boarding kennels can be pricey, and the cheaper ones may not offer the same level of care as the more expensive alternatives. Sometimes extra playtime and walks require an additional fee. Carefully research the boarding kennels in your area; read reviews and take a close look at what is included in the price. Also, look at how clean the environment is and how much time the dogs spend in cages versus in free-play areas.

If you decide a boarding kennel is not a good fit, you also have the option of hiring a pet sitter. You could hire a professional, or you could simply ask a neighbor to go over to your house a few times a day. Since this person will be in your home unsupervised, it is important that you trust whomever you hire. You should put the same amount of care into choosing a pet sitter as you would a babysitter.

Your Sheltie may be more comfortable being cared for in his own home, and he will receive more individualized attention. This can be an ideal option if you have other pets that need to be cared for as well. You can also ask the pet sitter to water your plants and bring your mail inside. Some are even willing to stay in your house overnight, so your dog has constant care and attention rather than being left alone.

There is no universally "right" decision when it comes to finding pet care while you're out of town. Do your research and figure out what would be best for you and your Sheltie based on his personality and the available options.

CHAPTER FIFTEEN
Senior Dog Care

It can be hard to accept that your precious fur baby isn't a puppy anymore, but as the years go by, you will start to notice some changes. He may be more content to sleep most of the day. He might not be able to run as fast or as long as he used to. You may even notice him wincing as he walks up the stairs. Age has its effects on dogs just as it does on people, and in order to give your Sheltie the quality of life he deserves, you will need to make some changes to accommodate his aging body.

Photo Courtesy of Britt Mertens

Shetland Sheepdogs generally have a lifespan of twelve to fifteen years, but they can be considered "senior dogs" starting around ten years old. This timeframe can vary depending on the individual dog, however. While some factors are outside of your control, such as your Sheltie's genetic predispositions, providing quality care throughout his life is the best way to ensure that he will live longer and remain healthier into his final years.

Grooming

Continuing to provide regular grooming is especially important as your Sheltie ages because his coat will become more brittle, and his skin will become dry and irritated if it isn't cared for properly. Regular brushing will prevent mats and tangles, which can become painful if neglected. Also, make sure you use a natural, nonirritating shampoo for sensitive canine skin. When you groom your Sheltie, run your hands over his body to feel for any unusual bumps. Older dogs are more at risk of cancer, and a Sheltie's long fur can easily hide developing tumors or skin conditions. Call your vet if you notice anything unusual. Many growths and lumps are benign, but it's always best to be safe. If there is a problem, early detection will improve the odds of any necessary treatment.

You will also need to make sure the fur around your Sheltie's anus remains clipped short, so the area remains clean. Senior dogs typically have more trouble defecating, and feces can easily get caught in long fur. Additionally, your Sheltie will still need the same seasonal haircuts and nail trimming as when he was younger.

Good dental health is also important. Many senior dogs lose some teeth if they did not receive proper dental care throughout their life. Make sure you regularly brush your Sheltie's teeth with an appropriate canine toothpaste to prevent tooth decay. Refer to Chapter Twelve for instructions on how to brush your dog's teeth.

Nutrition

"Purina Pro Plan makes a dog food for seniors called Bright Minds. I have seen this help seniors who have some cognitive Issues. I think it is always good to supplement with glucosamine. This helps the joints of older & more mature dogs."

SHERRY DEEDS
BellaRose Shelties

Many commercial dog foods claim to be formulated for senior dogs, but often this is just a marketing tactic. According to the AKC, there is currently no senior dog food recognized by the Association of American Feed Control Officials (AAFCO), so these foods may not have been tested for their efficiency or been proven to meet a senior dog's nutritional requirements[1]. These foods are not necessarily a bad choice, but make sure you look beyond the label to see what the food contains. Generally, any wholefood-based adult formulas are fine for senior dogs, as long as they meet the nutritional requirements. Older dogs need food that is easily digested, though, and if your Sheltie has trouble chewing, wet food might be the best option.

You may also need to adjust your Sheltie's caloric intake based on his reduced activity levels. Senior dogs can easily become obese if they no longer burn as many calories as they did in their youth but still eat the same amount of food. Talk to your vet to determine the type and amount of food that is best for your Sheltie as he ages. Also, if your Sheltie's appetite suddenly decreases, tell your vet because this might be a sign of a bigger health problem.

Exercise

Exercise will play a crucial role in maintaining your Sheltie's health as he ages. He likely won't have the same amount of stamina as before, but daily exercise will help minimize the negative effects of age by keeping his muscles strong and his mind sharp. Keep in mind that his joints might be painful, though, so let him set the pace and don't push him beyond his capabilities. Slow, gentle walks can provide a good opportunity to build strength and stamina since you can adjust the length and pace of the walk according to what your Sheltie can tolerate. Shelties aren't always fans of water, but if your pup enjoys it, swimming is also a good, low-impact form of exercise that is gentle on the joints.

If you allow your Sheltie to become too sedentary, his joints will become stiff, and his muscles will deteriorate, which will worsen his pain. His overall quality of life will decline, and his mood will likely suffer in addition to his physical health. He will be at much greater risk of obesity. His overall mobility will also become impaired, which will make exercising even harder, so it is important for your Sheltie to remain active from the beginning.

---

1   www.akc.org/expert-advice/nutrition/best-dog-food-small-breeds

Common Old-Age Ailments

Age can take a heavy toll on dogs. Their bodies start to wear down over the years, and they become more prone to various health conditions. Since older dogs are more at risk for certain diseases and parasites, you will need to start taking your Sheltie to the vet semi-annually rather than annually. Your vet will help you determine your Sheltie's level of health, catch any potential problems, and alter your plan of care as necessary.

Here are some common ailments your senior Sheltie might face and what you can do to help:

1. **Arthritis:** Joint pain is extremely common in older dogs as the cartilage wears away in their hips, shoulders, knees, and ankles. There is no cure for this condition, but you can talk to your vet about adding supplements, such as fish oil, to your Sheltie's diet to support joint health. You can also make your home more comfortable and accessible for your dog. For example, you can put steps next to your bed, so your Sheltie doesn't have to strain himself by jumping, and you can provide other comfy places for him to sleep, which might offer some relief.

2. **Loss of Hearing and Vision:** Just like humans, dogs can experience a loss of hearing and/or vision as they age. If these conditions are solely brought on by age, they cannot be cured; however, sometimes underlying issues, such as cataracts, can be treated surgically, and regularly cleaning the ears can help slow down hearing loss. If your Sheltie loses his hearing, you can train him to follow his usual commands through hand signals. You can also accommodate a loss of vision by avoiding rearranging the furniture in your house and by simply being extra patient with your pup.

3. **Cognitive Dysfunction:** Senior dogs can experience cognitive dysfunction similar to dementia or Alzheimer's disease in humans. Signs include disorientation or confusion, appearing lost in familiar places, whining or barking for no apparent reason, decreased interaction, and bathroom accidents. These can also be symptoms of other health problems, however, so speak to your vet to pinpoint the exact cause and figure out how to best support your Sheltie.

4. **Kidney Disease:** Many older dogs develop kidney disease, but if you catch it early enough, there are treatment options which can help manage the effects of the disease and improve the dog's quality of life, such as a prescription diet. Signs to watch for include increased urination and thirst, loss of appetite, nausea, and lethargy.

5. **Heart Problems:** If you notice any coughing, difficulty breathing, loss of consciousness, or unexplained vomiting, call your vet right away, as these might be signs of congestive heart failure. This is caused when the heart isn't able to pump blood effectively, so the chest becomes backed up with fluid.

6. **Cancer:** Sadly, cancer is all too common in senior dogs and is a leading cause of death in pets over ten years old. However, early detection can improve treatment outcomes, so regular screenings and checkups are important. Also, don't forget to get any unusual lumps checked out. Treatment options will vary depending on the type and stage of the cancer.

When It's Time to Say Goodbye

I'll be honest—I've been dreading writing this section. I don't want to think about a time when Winnie won't be around anymore. We all want to believe our pets will live forever, and when the end does come, it can be hard to fill that void.

Euthanasia

If your Sheltie starts to suffer from extreme pain or discomfort as he ages, you might face the difficult decision of euthanasia. If it's no longer possible to keep your Sheltie reasonably comfortable or maintain a good quality of life,

sometimes the kindest choice is to end his suffering. However, this decision can leave you wracked with guilt and conflicting emotions. On one hand, you don't want to see your Sheltie suffer any more, but on the other hand, you don't want to go through the pain of losing him any sooner than you have to. In this scenario, you will need to take a serious look at your dog's quality of life, discuss all your options with your vet, and choose what would be best for your Sheltie. If you decide euthanasia is the most humane route, you will need to allow time for everyone in your family to say goodbye. If you have children, you will need to explain what's going to happen in age-appropriate terms.

Your vet will explain the process to you, but feel free to ask for additional clarification if necessary. Often the vet will initially administer a sedative to keep the dog calm, then give the euthanasia medication through an IV in one of the dog's legs. While the medication might vary, most vets use a large dose of pentobarbital, a seizure medication that will render the dog unconscious. Within a couple minutes, the medication will gently shut down the dog's heart and brain functions. Sometimes the dog might make small, involuntary movements or urinate, or his eyes might not close completely. These are completely normal responses, and they do not mean that the dog is in pain. For the dog, the process simply feels like drifting off to sleep.

You will need to decide where you would like the procedure to take place. Some vets are willing to come to your house so your Sheltie can be in the comfort of his own home, or you have the option of going into the veterinary office. If you have other dogs, performing the procedure at home can help give them closure. Dogs are pack animals, so if one of them leaves and never comes home, they can become confused and continue to look for the missing member. However, if you have young children, it might not be appropriate for them to witness the process. Whether you stay home or go into the veterinary office is a completely personal decision. Likewise, you will have the choice of whether you stay with your Sheltie during the procedure or not. You might want to stay with him to comfort him in his last moments, but some people find that it's too emotionally difficult. Either way, you should bring a favorite blanket or bed for your Sheltie to lay on, especially if you go to the veterinary office, so he has something familiar and comforting with him.

After the procedure, you will need to decide how to lay your Sheltie to rest. If you want to bury him at home, you will need to check local regulations to ensure this is legal. Other options include going to a pet cemetery or cremation. Your vet will be able to give you guidance in making these next steps.

Grieving

No matter how the end comes, it won't be easy. After all, your Sheltie isn't just an animal. He's a member of your family, and he's your best friend. Losing him can feel like losing a piece of your heart. Your home will seem emptier. You might find yourself turning to pet him or say something to him

out of habit. You might expect to see him lying in his favorite spot and feel a rush of pain and loneliness when you find it empty.

You will need to give yourself time to grieve and allow yourself to cry as much as you need. Releasing your feelings is the only way you'll heal. It can also be helpful to find someone to talk to—perhaps a friend or family member who also knew and loved your Sheltie. Often comfort is found in community.

When you're ready, you can start to redirect your energy in a positive direction. Many people find that volunteer work can help them feel more at peace and fill the void in their heart after a loss. If you want to be around animals, you can try helping at your local humane society, or you can find another charity in your area that speaks to you.

Healing will take time, but have hope that things will get better eventually, even if it doesn't feel like it in the moment. As the months pass, the pain will start to subside, but the time you spent with your Sheltie will always remain a cherished memory. Ultimately, you can take comfort in the fact that you gave your Sheltie a good life, and just as he brought endless joy to your life, you were the primary source of happiness in his.

CONCLUSION

The journey of raising a Shetland Sheepdog from puppyhood until the end of his life is filled with laughter, frustration, love, comfort, and pain, but every moment is worth it all. Savor the time you have with your Sheltie. Go on that extra walk. Throw the tennis ball. Take the time to pet him, kiss his forehead, and tell him how much you love him.

If you're a new owner and are buying or adopting a Sheltie for the very first time, you have a lot to look forward to. No one loves more deeply or loyally than a Shetland Sheepdog, so take care of him and appreciate him. You will be his entire world, and he will change your life for the better. He deserves no less.

Now excuse me while I go hug Winnie...then beg her forgiveness for violating her personal space.

Printed in the USA
CPSIA information can be obtained
at www.ICGtesting.com
LVHW080046231123
764661LV00004B/386